COVER DESIGN

This symbol comes from the Ne shu Wa lo Shin ka or Little Rain Songs. In the ceremony, the ground is struck with a ceremonial club. Then from the dent made in the ground, a straight line is drawn to the west. This is followed by drawing a wavy line to the north from the dent. Next, a straight line is drawn to the east and finally a wavy line to the south.

There are three specific significances to this symbol. First, the seizure of the sky by the earth. Second, the path of the sun from sunrise to midday and thence to sunset. Third, the spreading of the sun's life-giving touch to the earth, to the left and right side of the path.

In a broader sense, it is a symbol of the unity of the tribe. Osage villages were laid out in a square. A central street ran east and west through the center and represented the sun's path. In the center stood the houses of peace, symbolized by the midday sun. To the left or north of the street were the Tsi shu [Sky People] clans, to the right were the Hun ka [Earth People] clans. The benefits of clan membership were symbolized by wavy lines.

OSAGE INDIAN

BANDS AND CLANS

BY

Louis F. Burns

CLEARFIELD

Originally published
Fallbrook, California, 1984

Reprinted for
Clearfield Company, Inc. by
Genealogical Publishing Co., Inc.
Baltimore, Maryland
2001

International Standard Book Number: 0-8063-5112-8

Made in the United States of America

Dedicated to

my Osage grandfather,

Louis Tinker

TABLE OF CONTENTS

LIST OF MAPS, DIAGRAMS, AND CHARTS

Maps

Diagrams

Charts

End Notes

PREFACE

In the spring of 1980, Mrs. Maudie Cheshewalla, Curator of the Osage Tribal Museum, expressed a need for a book to help Osages trace their paternal lineages. A revival of interest in the Osage practice of child naming creates a demand for proof of descent through the male lineage, to be sure of the proper clan. After some investigation into the matter, it became evident there was, indeed, a need for such a reference. Not only was there a need for an Osage family research reference, but there was a need for a source book in general Osage research.

After a period of examining what had been written about the Osages, several voids emerged. The foremost omission was studies of Osage Bands and Clans. There were fragments of band and clan information scattered throughout Osage literature. However, no concentrated source of such information was available. The absence of information about Osage mixed bloods was also noticeable. It would seem this area is a rich field for extensive research. A problem of language also surfaced; one does not do much Osage research without coming against the language barrier. Comprehension of Osage words is difficult, but trying to decipher the phonics of the many sources presents more than a challenge.

Decoding these phonics is a laborious task for those who have a working knowledge of the Osage language; for those without knowledge of the language, the task is impossible. The Osage language is related to the society from which it comes. One may read the translated name, Reaches the Sky without comprehending its meaning or things associated with it. Knowledge of Osage society would add the information, that, this is a name of the Isolated Earth clan. Other knowledge would tell the reader, this clan symbolized the isolation of the earth from other cosmic bodies, and they used the four winds as weapons. Without this knowledge one might assume the isolation refers to the people. Reaches the Sky refers to the wind, this and the use of the four winds as weapons suggests a relationship of this clan to the Elk and Four Winds clans. This is only a simple example to illustrate how knowledge of Osage society can enrich a researcher's fund of working information. Accurate identification of Osage persons, bands, clans, tribal divisions, and events are impossible without having some language and society data.

In the process of bringing band and clan information together in one source we have kept the non-researcher in mind. Readers who are interested in Indian lore will find much to attract them. We have made an effort to avoid sociological terms and other unusual academic terms. A special effort was made to write in clear readable English. This is also why all Osage words are written in the American spellings found in the Osage Annuity Rolls.

The material is organized by the size of tribal units. Tribes and divisions are presented first. We then move to the various bands. This is followed by the clans in their various circles. Next the individuals of the clans are presented followed by kinship terms. A special language table and bibliography conclude the general organization.

For clarification purposes, maps and diagrams have been added to enhance the text information. Sub-indexes were included to facilitate the use of tables and lists. We believe the general index will further increase the value of *Bands and Clans.*

THE PHYSICAL DIVISIONS
1800-1840

In the early accounts about the Osage, little attention was given to the gentile or clan organization. Almost all sources used the terms Big Osage, Big Hill or Big Bone and Little Osage or Little Bone. Except for the Bone terms, the names arise from the flood tradition.

The flood tradition relates that during a sudden flood the people were forced to flee to safety. Panic and the need for haste caused some mixing of the divisions and clans. That is, both Big Hills and Little Osages had representatives of most of the clans in their respective physical divisions. As a result of the flood, five distinctive physical divisions were created which crossed over and blended with some of the gentile divisions. In a majority of the records, there is no systematic use of the Big Hill and Little Osage terms. However, in general, three of the physical divisions were included in the Big Osage-Big Hill terms and two were included in the Little Osage term.

When the flood struck, some fled to the tops of the trees and were called Top of the Tree Sitters. Others sought safety among the trees on a hilltop and were called the Upland Forest People. A third group found haven among the thorny growth on the sides of a ravine; they were called Thorny Bush People. These first three groups were included in the terms, Big Osage and Big Hill. A variation in usage often appears in the accounts. The term Big Osage is used to denote the Top of the Tree Sitters and Thorny Bush People. Big Hill is then used to describe the Upland Forest People.

A fourth group was unable to reach high ground, but took refuge on the talus at the base of a cliff. For this reason, they were called the Down Under People. The last group stood on the hummocks of dry land amid the swirling flood-waters and were called Heart Stays People. These last two groups were included in the term Little Osage. It should be noted, some use this term to describe the Ft. Osage-Timber Hill bands of Heart Stays Osages. The other Little Osages, which included both Heart Stays and Down Under People, are then further described as White Hair's Band: Little Osage.

From the 1600's until allotment in 1906, these physical divisions tended to place their villages on terrain that matched the terrain which had been their salvation. For example, the Little Osages built their villages on river benches with a steep hill rising from the bench. These sites give us clues that help determine which physical division lived there, but they give little help in identifying the gentile divisions. Gentile divisions are best determined by the Chief's names and by the personal names used within the group.

We must return to the Bone terms since these are sometimes used in the early records. These names originate in a tradition about mastodons. From the descriptions in the legend, it is evident this event occurred after the great flood.

1

This was probably in the late 1500's or early 1600's[1]. For some unknown reason all the "large animals" had fled to the West across the Mississippi River. They gathered at the base of a hill below the Osage Village. There they fought each other until only the badly wounded animals were left alive. The Osages slew these wounded animals so none survived. Bones of these animals were found later by Europeans where the legend said they would be. Since these large bones were found around the spring used by the Big Hills and Big Osages these groups were called the Big Bone Osage. Only smaller bones were found near the Little Osage Villages so they were called Little Bone Osages.

The Jesuits followed the practices of their times and used the terms: Big Osage, Big Hill, Little Osage and Little Osage: White Hair's Band. Sometimes they gave the names of the Chiefs and thus, left some clue about the clan led by that Chief. Determining precisely which clan or clans were in each band would be a task far beyond the scope of this work. This would require translating the names recorded for a band and checking these translated names against a list of known clan names. Given a fixed system of phonics this would not be so difficult. However, the Jesuits were not consistent as individuals or as a group in their phonics. Thus, the task becomes overwhelming. We have tried to indicate the clan of the band when the evidence was readily available, for verification, in our list of Osage Towns mentioned in the Jesuit records of Osage Mission.

By 1802, the Osages were actually three separate tribes sharing the same gentile organization. These tribes were the Little Osages of the Missouri River, White Hair's Bands and Claremore's Bands. Various estimates place Claremore's Bands as being from one-third to one-half of the Osages. There is small doubt that they were the largest of the three tribes. In 1800, the Osage towns were scattered over Missouri, Arkansas, Kansas and Oklahoma. The majority were in Missouri clustered in two areas. Small villages which may have been merely hunting camps have been located in Oklahoma and Arkansas while others were certain to have been in Missouri and Kansas. It has been established, that, Black Dog's permanent town was near present-day Baxter Springs, Kansas before 1800.

The two concentrations in Missouri at the beginning of the nineteenth century were on the Missouri River watershed. There were six Little Osage Villages on either side of the Missouri River between Malta Bend and Glasgow, Missouri. Ft. d'Orleans was built in the northern bend of the Missouri River to serve the Missouris and Little Osages in this area. About 1802, the three villages on the north side of the river moved to the south side because of pressure from the southern Sac and Fox. After the Treaty of 1808, all these Little Osage bands moved to the area near Ft. Osage.

The junction of the Little Osage, Marmaton and Marais des Cygne-Osage Rivers had the largest concentration of Osage villages. There were at least eight villages in this area before 1800. Harmony Mission and Papinsville

2

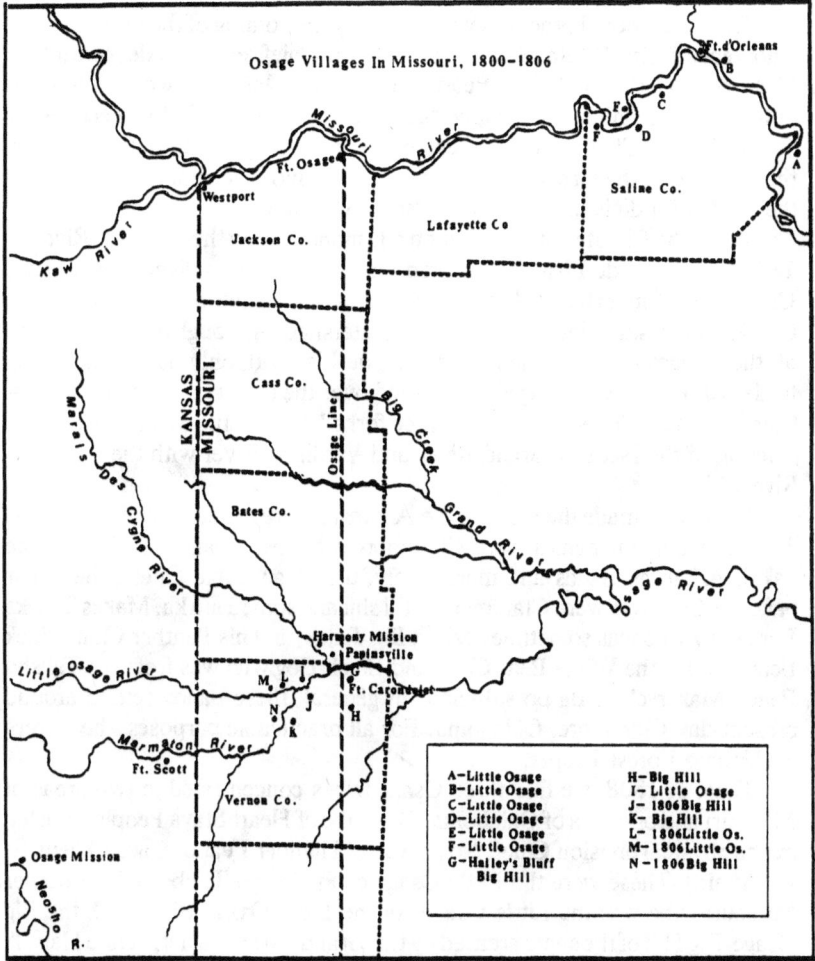

Osage Villages In Missouri, 1800-1806

A—Little Osage	H— Big Hill
B—Little Osage	I— Little Osage
C—Little Osage	J— 1806 Big Hill
D—Little Osage	K— Big Hill
E—Little Osage	L— 1806 Little Os.
F—Little Osage	M—1806 Little Os.
G—Halley's Bluff	N—1806 Big Hill
Big Hill	

3

were, of course, built here after 1800, but it was in this year that Ft. Carondelet was built at Halley's Bluff below the Big Osage village on top the bluff. Five of the eight towns were Big Osage towns and three were Little Osage towns.

Two Grand Chiefs were always selected to hold supreme power under the gentile organization. One Chief was usually dominent in practice, but in theory their power was equal. The two Grand Divisions were Tsi shu [Sky] and Hun ka [Earth]. The Grand Tsi shu Chief always came from the Tsi shu Peace Maker Clan while the Grand Hun ka Chief always came from the Pon ka Peace Maker Clan. About 1800, the traditional Grand Tsi shu Chief died, customarily his son, Claremore, would have become the Grand Tsi shu Chief[2].

These traditional practices were upset by the coming of the fur trade. The Chouteaus found White Hair, a Tsi shu clan Chief, easier to deal with than Claremore's father had been. Fearing that young Claremore would follow the policies of his father, they supported White Hair in his bid to become the Grand Tsi shu Chief. The Chouteau influence broke the tradition followed in the selection of the Grand Tsi shu Chief's. Claremore became a clan Chief but the seeds of a division among the Osages was sown.

When the Chouteaus lost the fur trade monopoly on the Missouri River, in 1802 to Manuel de Lisa, they looked for some means to divert the lucrative Osage trade. Since they still held the Arkansas watershed monopoly, they tried to cajole the Osages into moving to that watershed. Although they failed to get all the Osages to move, their efforts left de Lisa with only half of the Osage trade. Almost all the Osages dissatisfied over the selection of White Hair as Chief followed Claremore to the "three forks". This name was applied to the junction of the Neosho-Grand River and Verdigris River with the Arkansas River.

Those who made the move to the Arkansas were called by various names. The most popular names were Claremore's Bands, Chaneers [place of the oaks], Arkansas Bands and more rarely, the Changeable Ones. The major bands of Chaneers were Claremore's Tsi shu and some Hun ka, Makes Tracks Far Away who was sometimes called Big Track, and his Panther Clan; Black Bear who led the White Bear Clan, and Black Dog who was from the Tsi shu Peace Maker clan, Ba po sub-clan. In general, these bands settled around present-day Claremore, Oklahoma. For all practicable purposes, these were all Upland Forest People.

Thus, in 1808, we find three Osage tribes concentrated in two areas of Missouri and one area of Oklahoma. One tribe of Heart Stays People were led by the physical division Chief, No pa walla [Thunder Fear or Cause Them To Be Afraid]. These were the Little Osage of Ft. Osage-Timber Hill. Another Missouri tribe was the Little Osages of the Little Osage River with the Big Osage-Big Hill of the same area led by the Grand Tsi shu Chief, White Hair. A third tribe was the Chaneers led by the Big Hill Division Chief, Claremore.

4

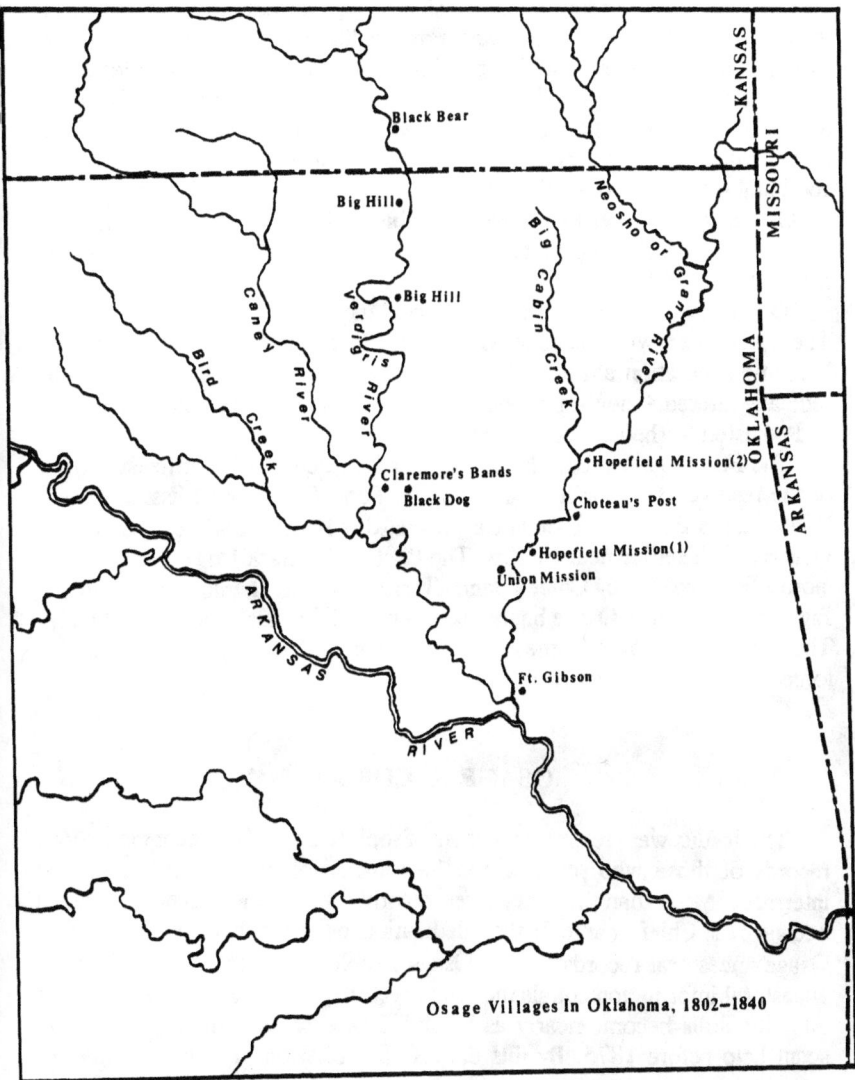

Black Bear

Big Hills

Big Hill

Caney River

Bird Creek

Verdigris River

Big Cabin Creek

Neosho or Grand River

KANSAS

MISSOURI

OKLAHOMA

ARKANSAS

Hopefield Mission(2)

Claremore's Bands

Black Dog

Choteau's Post

Hopefield Mission(1)

Union Mission

ARKANSAS

Ft. Gibson

RIVER

Osage Villages In Oklahoma, 1802–1840

These were residing between the three forks and the present Kansas-Oklahoma state line. Their towns were either along or between the Neosho-Grand and Verdigris Rivers.

Although Ft. Osage was not terminated until 1822, its operation was suspended during the War of 1812. This left Côte Sans Dessein, opposite the mouth of the Osage River, the westernmost outpost. Most of those who owned the Côte were French-Osage mixed-bloods, so they were partial to the Osages. However, the Côte was on the north side of the Missouri River which was a strong-hold of the southern Sac and Fox, traditional Osage enemies. Faced with the lack of protection and impossibility of trade in their current location, the Ft. Osage Little Osages decided to move to a more desirable area. In 1812, they joined the Chaneers and thus reunited for a short time, two of the three Osage tribes, at least territorially they were united. However, the almost continual warfare between the Chaneers and immigrant Cherokee caused the Ft. Osage Little Osages to remove to Timber Hill between Big Hill Creek and Labette Creek, Labette County, in Kansas. They made this move somewhere near the year of 1822.

During the early 1870's the Osages built the last of their traditional towns. These were the towns that ushered them into the mainstream of American life. Within a generation almost all the traditional Osage life was either gone or radically altered. They sought out their traditional terrain in the last reserve and adjusted to the new conditions.

The Ft. Osage-Timber Hill Little Osages settled in the Northeast portion of the reserve. They built their towns on Pond Creek and Mission Creek. White Hair's Big Hills settled near present-day Barnsdall while other White Hair Big Hills settled near Fairfax. The Big Hills of Black Dog's Band, Claremore's Band and Saucy Chief's Band all settled around Hominy. White Hair's Big Osage and Little Osage bands settled around Pawhuska and Gray Horse. The Osages were now at home in their final reserve. Never again would they be forced to leave their homes.

OSAGE RECORDS

The Jesuits were relentless seekers of souls to save. They kept meticulous records of those who received the Sacraments of baptism, marriage and interment. More than this, they often recorded where these events occurred and gave the Chief's name. In their dedication to their faith, they left the gift of Osage ancestoral records for the Osage People. No other source of Osage ancestoral information equals the Jesuit records. Only the U.S. Government Annuity Rolls become nearly as helpful. However, the Annuity Rolls give scant help before 1875. By this date, Osage Mission had closed. Between

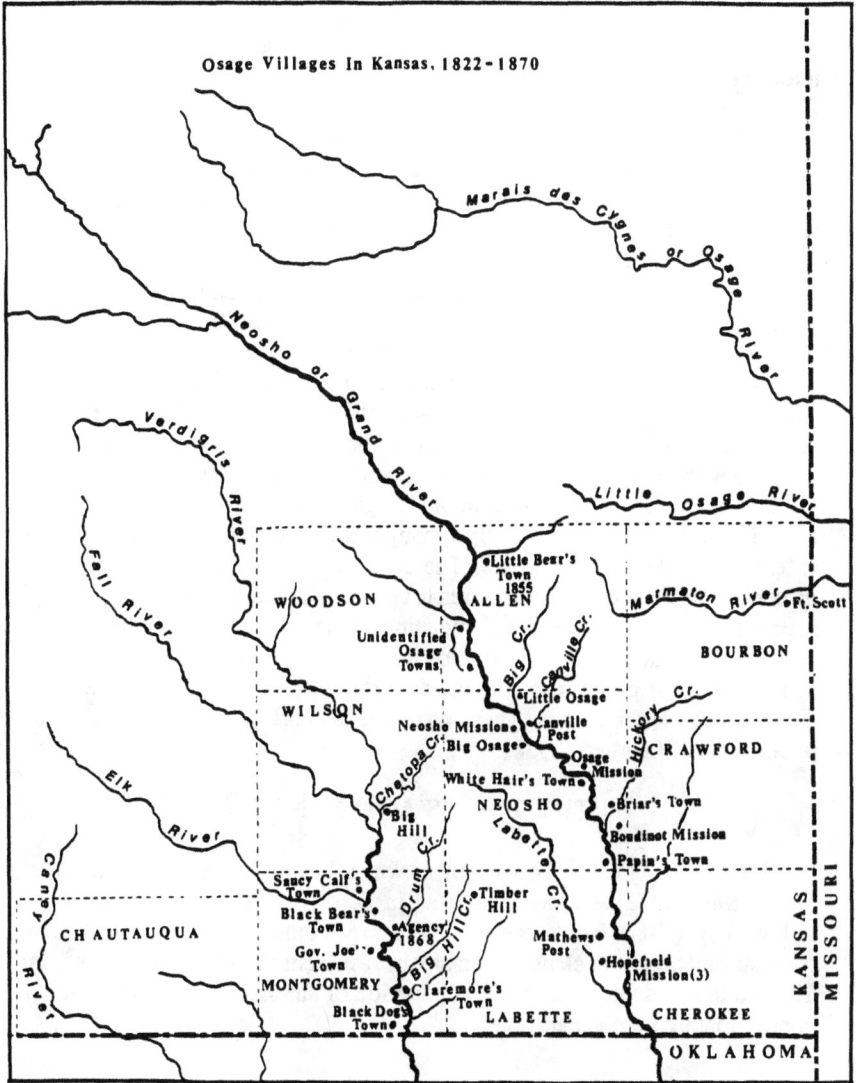

Osage Villages In Kansas, 1822-1870

1820 and 1872, the Osage Mission records remain the best source of information about Osage family members. From 1875 to 1900, the Annuity Rolls become the best source. Since 1900, the Agency records and the U.S. census become the best source. Researchers of Osages in general as well as Osage family researchers should be aware of several factors.

In 1897, all the Osage archives not then in current use were destroyed in a fire. This is a great handicap to any Osage research. A researcher must, therefore, seek alternate records. This requires a greater amount of multiple record use than would normally be required to acquire a desired piece of information. For example, the early Annuity Rolls, 1847-1874, give the Band, Head of Household, number of persons in the household, and dates roll was made. This information is vastly enhanced when worked with the information contained in the Osage Mission records. Likewise between 1875 and 1897, the Annuity Rolls are enriched by working them with the Haskell and Carlisle school records.

Another factor which complicates Osage research is inconsistencies in phonics. The only available system of consistent Osage phonics is Dr. Francis La Flesche's, *A Dictionary of the Osage Language,* Smithsonian, Bureau of American Ethnology, Bulletin 109. We cannot conceive how anyone could do a creditable Osage research project without having this reference available. The Annuity Rolls furnish the only system that uses English phonics. English sounds lack the precision of La Flesche's phonics, but they are the system in use among the Osage People. We have used the phonics of the Annuity Rolls throughout this book for this reason. Although the phonics of the Annuity Rolls are fairly consistent, they do vary among the various recorders and to some extent with individual recorders. The Jesuit's phonics are inconsistent to a disconcerting degree. One must often list pages of names before the patterns of syllables reveal their intended meaning. Even then, one is reluctant to conclude they have a correct rendition until it is confirmed in some other way. A final class of phonics is contained in the various accounts of travelers, explorers and letter writers. These often act as confirming sources insofar as phonics are concerned.

THE TOWNS AND BANDS

The following list of Osage Towns was taken from the Jesuit records of Osage Mission. These towns were all in Southeastern Kansas. This list is followed by a list of bands as given in the three Annuity Rolls of 1878. These two lists and the list of clans should aid the researcher in tracing the clans from 1800 to the present. This would be a period of almost two hundred years or approximately nine generations.

KANSAS

OKLAHOMA

ELGIN

Buck Creek

CANEY RIVER

Canville
Post

Hickory
Sta.

Strike Axe Band

Pond Creek

No pa walla
and Ne kah ke pah ne Bands

BOWRING

Mission Cr.

Saucy
Chief
Band

Sand Creek

PAWHUSKA
White Hair and Beaver
Bands

Big Chief
Band
BARNSDALL

Bird Creek

96th Meridian

Salt Creek

Big Hill
FAIRFAX

GRAY HORSE
Gov. Joe and
Tail Chief
Bands

Hominy Creek

HOMINY
Black Dog,
Claremore and
Saucy Calf
Bands

ARKANSAS

RIVER

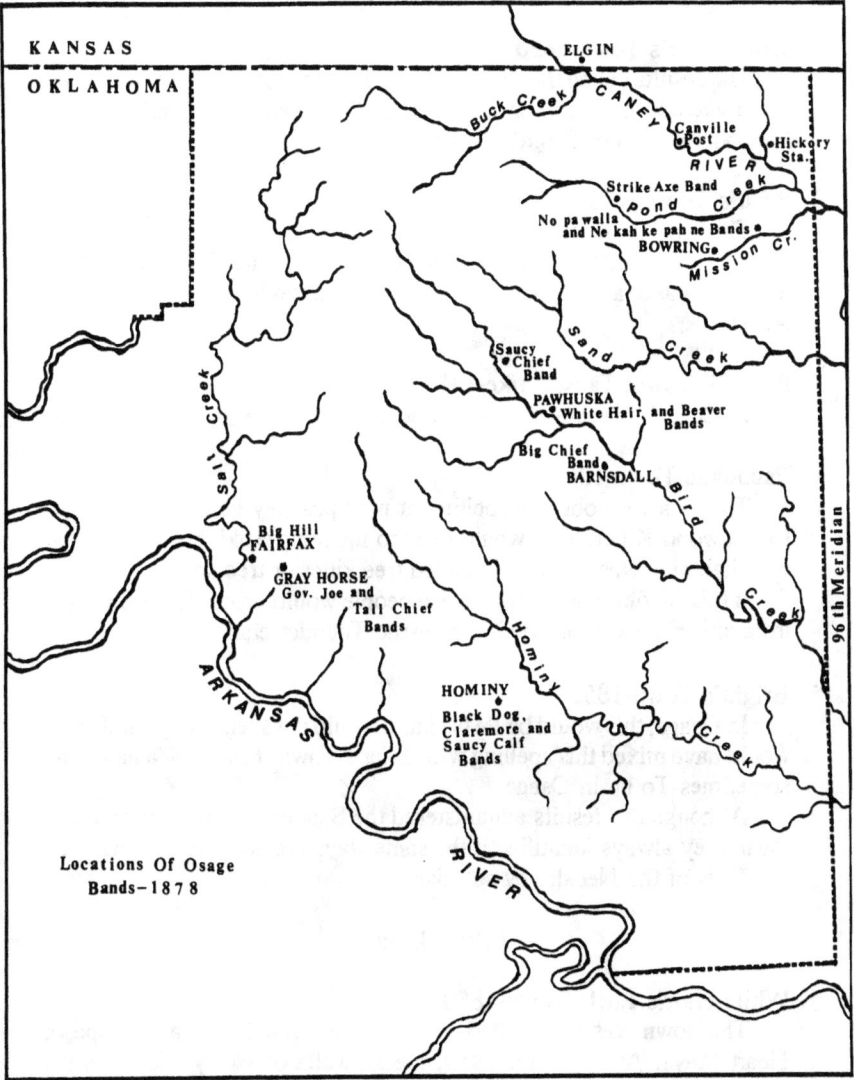

Locations Of Osage
Bands-1878

9

BANDS MENTIONED IN THE
JESUIT RECORDS

Neosho River

Big Hill

1. **White Hair's Town-1850**
   The Jesuits called this White Hair's Town because he lived there. Its name was No ne o pah or Peace Pipe. It was about five miles up the Neosho River from Papin's Town.

2. **Briar's Town-1852**
   This is also given as Whacha chingn's Town and Shopeshinca's Town. This would translate to Shop pe shin ka or Little Beaver. In 1859, this band was headed by Cuci nica which translates to Ka ke ne ka or Man Apart.

3. **Big Hill Town: Tanwa hike-1859**
   In English, Tanwa hike would be Tun ka He ka or Standing Chief.

4. **Paconkze Town-1860**
   This is a very obscure spelling, it may possibly be Pa ko ka che or Cottonwood Killer. This would refer to lightning striking a cottonwood tree; lightning was commonly called tree killer or tree splitter.
   If this rendition is correct, these people would probably be Big Hills from either the Cottonwood clan or the Thunder clan.

5. **Bright's Town-1852**
   In Osage, this would be Pe tse ka. It would not seem likely the Jesuits would have mixed this spelling with Briar's Town. Briar is Wa ha ke and sometimes To hu in Osage.
   Although the Jesuits administered the Sacraments frequently in this town, they always identified it the same way. We are placing it with the Big Hills of the Neosho by surmise.

Little Osage

6. **White Hair's Little Town-1850**
   This town was also called Papin's Town and Non tsa wah spa or Heart Stays. At this date, 1850, Ne ka walla or Noisy Man was the

10

Chief. The Jesuits spelled Heart Stays as Nantze waspe and Noisy Man as Nicanalla. Moh he ah gra or Reaches The Sky was an earlier Chief. This name refers to the wind, but Reaches The Sky is a name of the Isolated Earth Clan.

While the Jesuits classed this town as Big Hill, the name clearly tells us it was Little Osages who were among White Hair's people on the Osage and Little Osage Rivers in Missouri.

This town was on the right bank of the Neosho River five miles downstream from White Hair's Town. M. Melicourt Papin and Baptiste Mongrain (son of Noel Mongrain) were agents at the American Fur Company post located here. Considerable evidence suggests that this post was sold to John Mathews around 1841. However, lacking conclusive evidence to verify this, we have separated the towns as the Jesuits did.

7. **Little Osage: Little Town-1847**

This town was either near or at the John Mathews trading post between the Neosho River and the mouth of Labette Creek. The Little Osage bands of Timber Hill were in this same area but to the northwest. As mentioned in number six above, this town is very likely to be the same as Papin's Town.

8. **Woipoka also Whapocha Town or Big Creek-1849**

In English, this would be Wa po ka or Owl; the gray owl specifically. This band was also called Big Creek Little Osage.

9. **Neosho Town (near Shoal Creek)-1850**

We have no further clues about this band other than they were Little Osage on the Neosho River.

10. **Little Osage:Big Town-1849**

We have no further clues about this band except it was on the Neosho River.

11. **Little Osage: Big Chief's Town-1850**

In Osage, Big Chief would be Ki he ka tun ka. This is a gentile name in the Fish People clan.

12. **Little Osage: (Achita tanwha)-1850**

This would be Ah ke ta tun ka or Big Soldier in English. Ah ke ta is more accurately rendered as Protector, however, Soldier is more commonly used. This name belongs to the Men of Mystery clan of the Tsi shu Grand Division.

13. **Little Osage: Micio shinka Town-1858**
     This would be Me Ka shin ka or Little Coon in English.

14. **Little Osage: Farshert Town-1855**
     This spelling does not fit into any Osage phonics known to us.

15. **Little Osage: Catses sakie's Town-1850**
     This spelling does not translate into known Osage phonics. However, it does seem to have something to do with cattail rushes or being rendered unconscious.

16. **Mill Town: Inshapi ungri-1853**
     This name is somewhat of a puzzle. A literal translation would be En shop pe o gre or Those Who Came to the Beaver Stone in English. Possibly this means those who built their village near the mill stones or the mill (provided by Treaty). We are surmising that Beaver Stones refer to the mill stones.

17. **Minze Waspe-1854**
     The meaning is obscure because the Jesuits may have written "M" instead of "N". If they meant Non tsa wa spa, this would be Heart Stays. If they meant Men tsa wa spa, this would mean Heart Secret or Heart Hidden. We are inclined to believe they meant Heart Stays since Heart Hidden does not appear in other Osage literature.

18. **Zaiwacheougni Town-1849**
     The meaning of this is uncertain, but it could be Sa wa she o gre or Those Who Came to the Rush Birds. This would refer to a place where swans would swim among cattails. The old villages in Missouri were called The Place of the Swans. If our rendition is correct, these would probably be Little Osage of the Cattail clan. It does not seem probable that they would be Swan people because these were a part of the Puma or Panther clan which was with Claremore.

Timber Hill Little Osage

19. **Little Bear's Town-1861**
     In Osage, this would be Wa sop pe shin ka or Little Black Bear in English. This name was usually shortened to Little Bear. Little Bear is a name belonging to the Night People of the Tsi shu Sub-Division. The Jesuits seem to have placed them correctly as Little Osage. Like Che to pa, they went to Kansas about 1822.

12

20. Citopa Town-1856

Che to pa means Four Lodges, in English. This refers to a war party that destroyed four lodges of the enemy along with all the inhabitants. It is true that this was a band of Ft. Osage Little Osage along with Little Bear's band. The fact that they lived around Timber Hill with No pa walla's band confirms this fact. These three bands were distinctly separate from either the White Hair or Claremore bands except from 1812 to 1822.

21. Little Osage: Num pe wale's Town-1859

Num pe wale in English is No pa walla. Mathews renders this as Thunder Fear which conveys the meaning very well. It is sometimes rendered as Causes Them To Be Afraid. La Flesche renders it as Fear Inspiring. The name refers to thunder and the awe it inspired. No pa walla is a name belonging to the Men of Mystery clan. We know these Little Osages joined the Chaneers in 1812, but around 1822 they moved to Timber Hill. No pa walla the Elder was Chief of the Little Osages at Ft. Osage.

Verdigris

Big Hill-Claremore's Bands

22. Claymour's Town: Sanze ougrin-1850

Son tsa o gre would be Those Who Came to the Upland Forest in English. This town was also called Pashu ougrin; Pa shon o gre or Those Who Came to the Bend of the River in English. This refers to Claremore's town near present-day Claremore, Oklahoma. The name is commonly spelled Pasuga.

Claremore's gentile name was Gra moie. Mathews gives his name as Arrow Going Home. This is probably correct, but it would be a different name for Claremore other than Gra moie. Gra moie means Passing or Moving Hawk, although it is sometimes given as Walking Eagle. This name belongs to the Tsi shu Peace Maker clan, but Mathews places Claremore in the Hun ka Grand Division. Claremore had at least one other name which was To won ka ha or Town Maker, this too is a name belonging to the Tsi shu Peace Maker clan. We have not been able to find Arrow Going Home among the known clan names. We can only speculate that it was a special honor name bestowed upon Claremore or that it was a mis-interpretation. The Jesuits often called Claremore's son Town Maker.

13

23. Claymore's Band: Shonkie onhe's Town-1852

Shon ka o he or The Dog That Came refers to the fact that Black Dog came with the Chaneers in 1802. He was called Man ka shon ka or Cut With Axe Dog in honor of making the Black Dog Trail also called Manka Shonka Trail and second Buffalo Trail. Shon ka sop pe or Black Dog is a name belonging to the Tsi shu Peace Maker clan.

The Jesuits note that in 1851, Black Dog's son was Chief. They often called this town Big Hill: Passoni tanwa, Pa son tun ka or Big Cedar. This refers to the first Black Dog's Town where Claremore, Oklahoma now stands. The town's name is commonly spelled Pasona.

24. Black Dog's Band: Wolf's Town-1850

Two spellings of wolf are in use. First Shon ka, which means any member of the dog family. Last Sho me ka se, which means the gray wolf.

25. Tsho honka's Band-1859

The Jesuits spelled this name many ways. Tsi shu hun ka seems to be an accurate translation of the phonics. Sacred Tsi shu or Sacred Sky is the meaning of the name, which belongs to the Tsi shu Peace Maker clan.

26. Tally's Town: Sanze ougrin-1850

This would be Son tsa o gre or Those Who Came to the Upland Forest. Since two Chiefs in the same year were assigned this town, Son tsa o gre, we must conclude this meant two different towns and the name referred to the people by the Osage Upland Forest name rather than Big Hill.

Tally's gentile name was Ta hah ka he or Deer With Branching Horns. Tally was headman of the Little Male Deer clan and his name belongs to this clan.

27. Wascha ougrin tanwa-1852

This would be Wa scah o gre to won or Those of the White Bear Town in English. The White Bear clan included the Black Bear sub-clan.

28. Owasapy Town-1861

O wa sop pe would be the Male Black Bear in English. The Chief was usually called Black Bear. This clan was Big Hill and should not be confused with Little Bear's Little Osages. Little Bear and Black Bear are from two different clans.

29. Cicio ancha Town-1855

This was Saucy Calf's town, located between the Elk River and the Verdigris River.

14

30. **Tci cio hanka Town-1859**
    The phonics are very bad here. However, this would be Governor Joe's band. They were on the right bank of the Verdigris, below the Agency in 1868.

31. **Feully's Town (on Verdegris)-1850**
    The spelling does not fit into known Osage phonics. Being on the Verdigris justifies placing it with Claremore's Big Hills.

32. **Fairashiehie's Band: Big Hill-1859**
    This name does not translate into known Osage phonics. It was placed here by conjecture.

BANDS LISTED IN THE
ANNUITY ROLLS OF 1878

1. **Big Chief Band**
    These are Osages of the White Hair bands. It has been said they are Upland Forest, Big Hills, who stayed with White Hair. Some say they were Little Osages. They settled at Barnsdall, formerly Big Heart, Oklahoma.

2. **Joe's Band**
    This is probably Governor Joe's Band. The band was Big Hill and had earlier been one of White Hair's bands. They settled near Gray Horse, Oklahoma. They were probably Upland Forest Big Hills.

3. **Big Hill Band**
    This is probably White Hair's, Big Hills who were led by Standing Chief in 1859. These were probably Upland Forest Big Hill Osage. They settled near Fairfax, Oklahoma.

4. **White Hair Band**
    These probably are both Big Osage and Little Osage with Thorny Bush, Big Osage in the majority. They settled in the present reservation near Silver Lake (South of Bartlesville, Oklahoma) at first. Since this was on the Cherokee Reserve they had to move again. They moved to the area around Pawhuska, Oklahoma.

5. **Tall Chief Band**
    These are Big Hills, probably of the Buffalo Bull clan. Earlier they were among the White Hair bands. They settled around Gray Horse, Oklahoma.

6. **Black Dog Band**

These are Upland Forest, Big Hill, Chaneers. They settled at Hominy, Oklahoma.

7. **Saucy Chief Band**

These are Heart Stays, Little Osage. They should not be confused with Saucy Calf's Big Hills. Saucy Chief's band settled in the Bird Creek bottoms north of Pawhuska, Oklahoma. They were probably part of White Hair's bands.

8. **Beaver Band**

These are probably White Hair's Big Osages or Brian's Band. They are Thorny Bush people. This band settled around Pawhuska, Oklahoma.

9. **Strike Axe Band**

This is a Little Osage band. They are probably Che to pa's Band. In any case, they are Ft. Osage-Timber Hill Little Osages or Heart Stays people. They settled in Osage County, Oklahoma on Pond Creek. The village was less than a mile upstream from the Pond Creek bridge on Highway 99. This was also a campsite on the Second Buffalo Trail or Black Dog Trail. A double cabin government distribution station stood here until the 1930's. The A. B. Canville trading post was on the Caney River two miles east of this village. The Pond Creek Station and Hickory Station were government ration distribution posts for the Little Osages.

10. **No pa walla Band**

This is a Ft. Osage-Timber Hill, Little Osage band. They are Heart Stays people. These people settled on Mission Creek northeast of Bowring, Oklahoma. Hickory Station was near the mouth of Hickory Creek on the Caney River about five miles north of this village.

11. **Ne kah ke pah ne Band**

These seem to be Ft. Osage-Timber Hill, Heart Stays, Little Osage. It was likely that this was Little Bear's Band in 1861. The Chief's name could be Ne ka ah ke pa ne or Runs To Meet Men. These people settled on Mission Creek northeast of Bowring, Oklahoma.

12. **Claremore Band**

These are Upland Forest, Big Hill, Chaneers. They settled at Hominy, Oklahoma.

13. Wah ti an kah Band

This would be Saucy Calf. These are Upland Forest, Big Hill, Chaneers. They were probably Tally's Band at one time. This is not the same band as Saucy Chief or Ki he ka wa ti an kah. Saucy Calf's band settled at Hominy, Oklahoma.

14. William Penn Band

This was a very small band. No reliable information was available to place them accurately. The Penns were in the White Hair Band in Kansas.

15. Half Breed Band

These were Osages who did not live in the traditional Osage manner. Practically all of them were mixed-bloods. It must be noted, however, that many mixed-bloods lived the traditional Osage life at this time and were not included in this band. Conversely, a few full-bloods who did not live the traditional Osage life were included in the half-breed band.

THE OSAGE MIXED BLOODS

The French term, metis, meant an Osage-French mixture. Half breed is a broader, but much abused term. If one took the term literally, it would mean a person who was half Osage and half some other blood. In common usage, it meant a person with any quantum of white blood. However, it also carried the stigma of denoting an inferior person. Metis and half breed are either debasing or too restrictive to meet our needs.

Among the Osage, the term mixed blood has a specific meaning; in the American culture, it is a general term. As used by the Osage, mixed blood denotes a person who is Osage and Caucasian. It does not encompass the broader meaning of national as well as other racial mixtures. We will use the term in the Osage sense. That is, we will not include Osage mixtures with other Indians without adding Indian, nor will we include mixtures of Osage and Negro. In the latter case, there is only one family of Osage-Negro origin in the tribe. Mixture of Osage and other Indians is widespread so we will touch on them as Osage-Indian mixed bloods.

A search of Osage literature will reveal a drought of information about Osage mixed bloods. It is surprising that no scholar has directed themselves toward the role of mixed bloods in general and in particular, the Osage mixed bloods. A researcher will find many allusions to the mixed blood such as, "...and three Frenchmen," or "...he was a good guide, for a half breed." Questionable reliability ranging from omission of names and patronizing statements, to outright negative comments with little basis in fact, are all too common. Yet, a researcher does sometimes find factual information as displayed in Ovid Bell's, Côte Sans Dessein. As one reads the various eye witness accounts of the Battle of Côte Sans Dessein, the heroic ingenuity of the Osage-French women and lone man defending the fort stands out. It causes one to wonder how Francis Parkman could infer, that, French women did not go out on the frontier with their men as the English women did.[3] He could not have gotten the idea from the French women who went with their men to Montreal and then to the outposts of Vincennes, Kaskaskia and Cahokia. What we are saying is, there lies a whole new perspective of American Frontier History waiting for a bright young mind to explore.

Has no student of the American Fur Trade noticed how successful the French and Scots were, in comparison with English and American traders? If one were to list the most successful fur companies and their fur collecting personnel, they would almost surely discover the French and Scots at the base of success. The answer, in part, lies in bias toward the Indian and mixed blood French. French and Scottish people clearly had less bias than the English and Americans. Bias is present in the literature, their acts, their attitude, and the failures of English and American companies who did not include French, Scots, and mixed bloods among their personnel.

Indians of the American mid lands had a marked preference for the French. Among the Osage, as late as 1880, French was still the preferred European language. The Osage preference can also be seen in their choice of missionaries. Although the American Board of Commissioners for Foreign Missions had an early start among the Osage, they failed to hold Osage hearts. They labored diligently and established many missions, but in less than a generation passed from the Osage scene. Only the French Jesuits were able to capture Osage hearts. This was not because of doctrine differences, but a difference in attitude between American Ministers and French Jesuits. An examination of the writings of these two missionary groups will reveal the different attitudes they had toward the Osage. While the Osage of that day were not usually literate, they were exceptionally adept at reading facial and body language.

Another unexplored area in American Frontier History is the role of mixed blood groups in Indian affairs. Their contrasted influence among the various tribes constitute a whole area of study. We believe the Osage-French would emerge as a unique group of mixed bloods. Their long existence among the Osage people suggest this possibility. They were a numerically significant group within the tribe by 1750. Isolation from other French-American cultures, initiated by the end of the French and Indian War in 1763, was insured by the Louisiana Purchase. The Osage-French, like the Osage full bloods were biased against Americans. They considered the American culture to be the most inferior culture known to them in 1803.

Unlike the American-Cherokee culture, the Osage-French culture did not fit into American thought habits. This becomes clear in a comparison of Osage successes when dealing with the French and their failures in dealing with the Americans. The long wars with the Cherokee also show the skillful hands of the American-Cherokee in contrast to the inept efforts of the Osage-French when dealing with Americans. The Cherokee and their mixed bloods were not more capable than the Osages and their mixed bloods. Capability, in this sense, follows thought patterns in a meeting of two alien cultures. Osage thoughts were directed through Osage and French concepts; Cherokee thoughts were directed through Cherokee and American concepts. Since American culture held dominion over both tribes, it was natural for the Americans to side with the American-Cherokee over the alien Osage-French. However, another factor was also involved in this matter, this was the different roles played by the American-Cherokee and Osage-French within their respective tribes. American-Cherokees often held Cherokee leadership positions while the Osage-French never held such positions until after 1870. At best, their tribal position was advisory, at the worst they were considered to be American allies by the Osage full bloods. We do not offer these thoughts as theories, but to expose a need for research in a neglected area.

The French who intermarried with the Osage were provincial French. They had neither the polish nor the frivolity of a Parisian. Often they were swaggering and boastful; traits that were not out of place in the Osage villages. Like the Osages, they were proud and had a strict code for living. Provincial French were not schooled in the art of masking their emotions and this lack caused some hardships for them among the Osage full bloods who were masters of masked emotions. The French, like most Caucasians, throw their toes outward when they walk or stand. Osages walk and stand with their toes pointed in the direction of travel or facing direction. This trait was comical to the Osage full bloods and they often mimicked, like Charlie Chaplin, the gait of the Osage-French who walked with the toes outward. This and eye coloration was a cause of friction between full bloods and mixed bloods. The full bloods were brown eyed, but many of the mixed bloods had grey eyes with brown flecks. Among all Osages, "pea-eye" was an insult which usually led to fights among the young men. Perhaps we should mention that the peas known to the Osage were grey with brown spots on them.

Only a few sources mention the moral strictness of the Osage-French. More commonly the loose ways of the Couer de Bois is stressed, probably because most Americans did not know the difference between a "woods beast" and a habitant. A Couer de Bois was roughly comparable to the American woods runner or long hunter. We say roughly, because the American culture reluctantly accepted their woods runners, socially. The Osage-French habitats did not accept their Couer de Bois socially, they were social outcasts. Unwed Osage-French daughters were never permitted to go about unchaperoned. Young men and women were not permitted to sit together at parties. They danced together only under the watchful eyes of their mothers.

Osage-French men permitted no liberties where their women were concerned. Louis Roy was so angry at the suggestion that his wife, Julia Royer, be presented with a silver urnial, to honor her for saving the fort at Côte Sans Dessein, that he refused to accept a silver mounted rifle, honoring him for his part in the same battle. The young men of St. Louis could not smooth over the old man's outraged sense of propriety. If Osage-French parents failed to prevent misconduct, the Priests did not fail to note it. The Jesuit Fathers kept a strict eye on their Osage-French flock. Any deviation from the code of Catholic doctrine was duly recorded in their registers. No one should ever believe these mixed bloods were loose in their morals. If they had not been a people of strong moral fiber, the full bloods would not have permitted intermarriage. Osage code of conduct was severe and only those with similiar codes were peremitted to marry within the tribe. Only four Americans met this harsh code before 1840. These were a Protestant missionary, a sergeant of the Lewis and Clark Expedition and two missionary blacksmiths.

Osage-French were an orderly people, commonly a syndic or clerk to keep the records was the only official in their villages. One can understand their dismay when exposed to the tumultuous Americans and a multitude of officials. Among the mixed bloods the lines were clearly drawn between right and wrong. One lived by the rules or became a Couer de Bois, an exile from the community.

One Osage-French custom can be upsetting to an Anglo minded researcher. They shared with the French of the mid Mississippi area and the Osage full bloods the use of dit names. These were not mere aliases but special names for individuals. Nicholas Royer I dit Sans Quartier and his son Nicholas Royer II dit Colas are typical examples of dit names. Others are Carboneaux dit Revelette, Louis Bartholet dit Grand Louis, Louis Prue dit Petit Louis, Jeanot dit La Chapelle and many others. Almost every Osage-French family is either known by a dit name today or has used a dit name in the past. Related to the problem of the dit name is another custom which is a less severe problem to researchers. Men and women who were especially notable, were always referred to by their surnames only. It was a way of showing respect for character, the thought being, everyone knew such an outstanding individual hence use of a given name was unnecessary. The wife of such a man was addressed as madam followed by her husband's surname. No title preceded or followed the outstanding individual's surname, it stood alone. While morals and customs reveal much about a people, they tell little about their locations.

A majority of the Osage-French families came from the French provinces occupied by American troops in W.W. I. These are the Chateau-Thierry, Belleau Wood, and Meuse-Argonne sectors of the Western Front. They came to Ville Marie in the Grand Recruitment of 1653 and changed the name of their new home to Montreal. One or possibly two Osage-French families were Acadians who were transported to the West Indies, Mobile, and New Orleans. Other Osage-French came direct from France or Montreal via the West Indies and New Orleans with Le Moyne. They built their solid houses and neat villages where they raised large families of sturdy men and women. These, in turn, voyaged on the great rivers of America and raised their families. Whole villages were established wherever they settled. They did not spread across the land and spoil the hunting for the Indian.

Two major portage routes led them south from Montreal, one was the Georgian Bay-Green Bay route to the Mississippi. The other was the Georgian Bay-Maumee River-Wabash River route to the Ohio. They established Vincennes at the mouth of the Wabash; Kaskaskia at the mouth of the Ohio along with Ft. Chartes; and Cahokia opposite the mouth of the Missouri. From New Orleans they came up the Mississippi and built St. Genevieve. At the end of the French and Indian war, St. Ange de Belrive surrendered Ft. Chartes to Major Sterling and his highlanders. St. Ange with his detachment and many habitants moved to the newly founded St. Louis. Most of the French of the Illinois country then built St. Charles above Portage des Sioux, by this time Cahokia had been washed into the Mississippi. In the next generation, the Osage-French founded Côte Sans Dessein at the mouth of the Osage River and the settlement which became Westport and then Kansas City.

In 1823, the Osage-French were scattered among settlements such as St. Louis, Florissant, St. Charles Côte Sans Dessein, Papinsville, and Westport in Missouri. A few were at Chouteau's Post on the Grand Saline in Oklahoma. Between 1825 and 1850 they were concentrated around Canville's Post, Osage Mission (now St. Paul), White Hair's Village, Papins town, and Mathew's Post on Labette Creek, all in Kansas on the Neosho River.

After removal from Kansas to the present reservation, in 1870, they settled in three areas. Most settled in the Strike Axe district on the Big Caney, next to the Kansas line. Another large group settled on the Arkansas east of present day Ponca City. A smaller third group settled on the Arkansas between Hominy and Tulsa. It must be borne in mind that about one-third of the Osage-French lived with the various bands. As a further comment, it must also be noted, that as townsites were developed, most of the mixed bloods moved to the new townsites.

OSAGE-INDIAN MIXED BLOODS

The rapid population growth and consequent expansion of the Algonquin and Siouan peoples have intrigued ethnologists. Smithsonian ethnologists have theorized that much of the population growth came from absorption of other tribes as the Sioux moved westward.[4] Certainly the Osage legends would tend to support this theory. In addition, recorded history indicates the Osages did follow the practice of absorbing other tribes as well as single individuals.

With the outbreak of the War of 1812, Ft. Osage suspended operations. The Missouris north of the Missouri River had been reduced to only seven lodges through constant warfare with the Sac and Fox. Without the protection of Ft. Osage, it was clear they would be totally destroyed. With this in mind, three lodges joined the Osage and four lodges joined their Chiwere Sioux cousins, the Otoe. W. J. McGee, in the Smithsonian Bureau of Ethnology, 15th Annual Report, states five or six lodges joined the Osages. Other accounts say three lodges. If we take the usual twenty to thirty persons per lodge as a basis of estimation, the Osage-Missouris would have been approximately seventy-five in number. These Missouris settled among White Hair's Little Osages on the Little Osage River.

No large scale absorption of non-Siouan Indians has come to our attention. Numerous adoptions of non-Sioux individuals are in the records. This is especially true of the Pawnee. Adoptions can lead to errors and mixed-up information. A classic example of possible misinformation is the case of Joseph Revard III. Some accounts give Joseph Revard, who was killed by the Cherokee on the Grand Saline, as being the son of a Pawnee mother who was an adopted Osage. Yet, his baptism record gives his mother as Catherine, an Osage woman. This does not necessarily mean she was Osage by birth, but it does throw a shadow across the claim she was Pawnee by birth. A provable error in connection with this Joseph Revard is the claim he was married to a Pawnee wife who was an adopted Osage. This Joseph Revard was married to Françoise Roy who was pure French from a proven lineage. Confusion probably arose because Joseph Revard III, of whom we have written, was the son of Joseph Revard II and grandson of Joseph Revard I. Joseph Revard III also had a son, Joseph Revard IV, and several grandsons named Joseph Revard. As a matter of passing interest, Joseph Revard III was a maternal great grandfather of Major General C. L. Tinker, for whom Tinker AFB is named.

The larger absorptions of other Indians by Osages have come from kindred Dhegiha Siouan tribes. There are large infusions of Konza (Kaw) and Quapaw blood among the Osage. Some Ponca and less Omaha blood is also present. After 1880, there was a sharp increase in the number of Osage-Potawotomi marriages. Some Osage-Cherokee mixtures were present as early as 1850 along with early Potawotomi and Kickapoo marriages. By 1880, the impact of Indian schools at Haskell and Carlisle were becoming evident in mixed marriages as well as education. The Osage-Indian mixed bloods are probably nearly as numerous as other mixed bloods, while a pure blood Osage has become a rarity.

23

CHART FOR CALCULATING QUANTUM OF OSAGE BLOOD

Osage	Non-Osage	1/16	1/8	3/16	1/4	5/16	3/8	7/16	1/2
1/16	1/32	1/16	3/32	1/8	5/32	3/16	7/32	1/4	9/32
1/8	1/16	3/32	1/8	5/32	3/16	7/32	1/4	9/32	5/16
3/16	3/32	1/8	5/32	3/16	7/32	1/4	9/32	5/16	11/32
1/4	1/8	5/32	3/16	7/32	1/4	9/32	5/16	11/32	3/8
5/16	5/32	3/16	7/32	1/4	9/32	5/16	11/32	3/8	13/32
3/8	3/16	7/32	1/4	9/32	5/16	11/32	3/8	13/32	7/16
7/16	7/32	1/4	9/32	5/16	11/32	3/8	13/32	7/16	15/32
1/2	1/4	9/32	5/16	11/32	3/8	13/32	7/16	15/32	1/2
9/16	9/32	5/16	11/32	3/8	13/32	7/16	15/32	1/2	17/32
5/8	5/16	11/32	3/8	13/32	7/16	15/32	1/2	17/32	9/16
11/16	11/32	3/8	13/32	7/16	15/32	1/2	17/32	9/16	19/32
3/4	3/8	13/32	7/16	15/32	1/2	17/32	9/16	19/32	5/8

13/16	13/32	7/16	15/32	1/2	17/32	9/16	19/32	5/8	21/32
7/8	7/16	15/32	1/2	17/32	9/16	19/32	5/8	21/32	11/16
15/16	15/32	1/2	17/32	9/16	19/32	5/8	21/32	11/16	23/32
4/4	1/2	17/32	9/16	19/32	5/8	21/32	11/16	23/32	3/4
1/32	1/64	3/64	5/64	7/64	9/64	11/64	13/64	15/64	17/64
3/32	3/64	5/64	7/64	9/64	11/64	13/64	15/64	17/64	19/64
5/32	5/64	7/64	9/64	11/64	13/64	15/64	17/64	19/64	21/64
7/32	7/64	9/64	11/64	13/64	15/64	17/64	19/64	21/64	23/64
9/32	9/64	11/64	13/64	15/64	17/64	19/64	21/64	23/64	25/64
11/32	11/64	13/64	15/64	17/64	19/64	21/64	23/64	25/64	27/64
13/32	13/64	15/64	17/64	19/64	21/64	23/64	25/64	27/64	29/64
15/32	15/64	17/64	19/64	21/64	23/64	25/64	27/64	29/64	31/64
17/32	17/64	19/64	21/64	23/64	25/64	27/64	29/64	31/64	33/64
19/32	19/64	21/64	23/64	25/64	27/64	29/64	31/64	33/64	35/64

21/32	21/64	23/64	25/64	27/64	29/64	31/64	33/64	35/64	37/64
23/32	23/64	25/64	27/64	29/64	31/64	33/64	35/64	37/64	39/64
25/32	25/64	27/64	29/64	31/64	33/64	35/64	37/64	39/64	41/64
27/32	27/64	29/64	31/64	33/64	35/64	37/64	39/64	41/64	43/64
29/32	29/64	31/64	33/64	35/64	37/64	39/64	41/64	43/64	45/64
31/32	31/64	33/64	35/64	37/64	39/64	41/64	43/64	45/64	47/64

CHART FOR CALCULATING QUANTUM OF OSAGE BLOOD

Osage	9/16	5/8	11/16	3/4	13/16	7/8	15/16	4/4
1/16	5/16	11/32	3/8	13/32	7/16	15/32	1/2	17/32
1/8	11/32	3/8	13/32	7/16	15/32	1/2	17/32	9/16
3/16	3/8	13/32	7/16	15/32	1/2	17/32	9/16	19/32
1/4	13/32	7/16	15/32	1/2	17/32	9/16	19/32	5/8
5/16	7/16	15/32	1/2	17/32	9/16	19/32	5/8	21/32

3/8	15/32	1/2	17/32	9/16	19/32	5/8	21/32	11/16
7/16	1/2	17/32	9/16	19/32	5/8	21/32	11/16	23/32
1/2	17/32	9/16	19/32	5/8	21/32	11/16	23/32	3/4
9/16	9/16	19/32	5/8	21/32	11/16	23/32	3/4	25/32
5/8	19/32	5/8	21/32	11/16	23/32	3/4	25/32	13/16
11/16	5/8	21/32	11/16	23/32	3/4	25/32	13/16	27/32
3/4	21/32	11/16	23/32	3/4	25/32	13/16	27/32	7/8
13/16	11/16	23/32	3/4	25/32	13/16	27/32	7/8	29/32
7/8	23/32	3/4	25/32	13/16	27/32	7/8	29/32	15/16
15/16	3/4	25/32	13/16	27/32	7/8	29/32	15/16	31/32
4/4	25/32	13/16	27/32	7/8	29/32	15/16	31/32	4/4
1/32	19/64	21/64	23/64	25/64	27/64	29/64	31/64	33/64
3/32	21/64	23/64	25/64	27/64	29/64	31/64	33/64	35/64
5/32	23/64	25/64	27/64	29/64	31/64	33/64	35/64	37/64

	25/64	27/64	29/64	31/64	33/64	35/64	37/64	39/64
7/32	25/64	27/64	29/64	31/64	33/64	35/64	37/64	39/64
9/32	27/64	29/64	31/64	33/64	35/64	37/64	39/64	41/64
11/32	31/64	31/64	33/64	35/64	37/64	39/64	41/64	43/64
13/32	29/64	33/64	35/64	37/64	39/64	41/64	43/64	45/64
15/32	33/64	35/64	37/64	39/64	41/64	43/64	45/64	47/64
17/32	35/64	37/64	39/64	41/64	43/64	45/64	47/64	49/64
19/32	37/64	39/64	41/64	43/64	45/64	47/64	49/64	51/64
21/32	39/64	41/64	43/64	45/64	47/64	49/64	51/64	53/64
23/32	41/64	43/64	45/64	47/64	49/64	51/64	53/64	55/64
25/32	43/64	45/64	47/64	49/64	51/64	53/64	55/64	57/64
27/32	45/64	47/64	49/64	51/64	53/64	55/64	57/64	59/64
29/32	47/64	49/64	51/64	53/64	55/64	57/64	59/64	61/64
31/32	49/64	51/64	53/64	55/64	57/64	59/64	61/64	63/64

THE OSAGE INDIAN GENTILE ORGANIZATION

So far as is known, no complete list or count of the various clan groups exists. A total of eighty-four are listed here. In all probability, the clans with their many subdivisions could be more than one hundred. The listed twenty-four clans appear to be complete since they are confirmed in the tribal circle count and participation in ceremonies. Sub-clans and sub-sub-clan listings are almost certain to be incomplete, because several important clans do not have any sub-clans listed. Other clans have fewer sub-clans than would seem warranted by their standing in the tribe.

In the Osage legends, a story of creating the Osage tribe is given. Wah kon ta told the Sky People [Tsi shu] and the Water People [Wah sha she] to search the world for the Earth People [Hun ka]. They were told to teach the Earth People the proper way to live. Since there were seven Sky People clans, seven Water People clans, and seven Earth People clans, incorporation of the seven Earth People clans would unbalance the traditional fourteen fireplaces in the Osage Tribal Circle. To maintain the symbolism of the original fourteen fireplaces the Sky People kept their seven fireplaces on the left half of the circle. To keep seven fireplaces on the right half of the circle, the Water People were counted as two fireplaces and the Earth People were counted as five fireplaces.

The Symbolic Order numbers the Sky Division from one through seven and the Earth Division from eight through fourteen. Under this arrangement, the clans were: (1) Tsi shu wearing a tail on the head; (2) Buffalo-bull face; (3) Sun carriers; (4) Tsi shu peacemaker; (5) Night people; (6) Buffalo-bull; (7) Thunder being; (8) Elder Osage; (9) Hunka apart from the rest; (10) Ponca peacemaker; (11) White eagle or Hun ka having wings; (12) Having black bears; (13) Elk; (14) Kon sa or Winds.

This fourteen clan order is easily confused with the three full twenty-four clan orders. Alignment of the clans is entirely different between the fourteen and twenty-four clan orders. In our presentation we have followed the twenty-four clan order so that all the clans can be shown.

The gentile organization of the Osage tribe had two grand divisions, the Tsi shu and Hun ka. These were divided into five sub-divisions; the first as Hun ka u tah nun tse, the second as Wha sha she, the third as the Hun ka sub-division, the fourth as Tsi shu and the fifth as Tsi ha she sub-division. A departure from the customary numbering has been made in this list. For convenience the clans are numbered from one through twenty-four. In the customary numbering, the Hun ka u tah nun tse are lettered with "C" followed by the Wah sha she which is numbered from one through seven, then the Hun ka numbered from one through seven, and the Tsi shu numbered from one through seven, the Tsi ha she are then lettered "A" and "B". The four diagrams shown in figures 1, 2, 3 and 4 show the four different orders of the tribal circle.

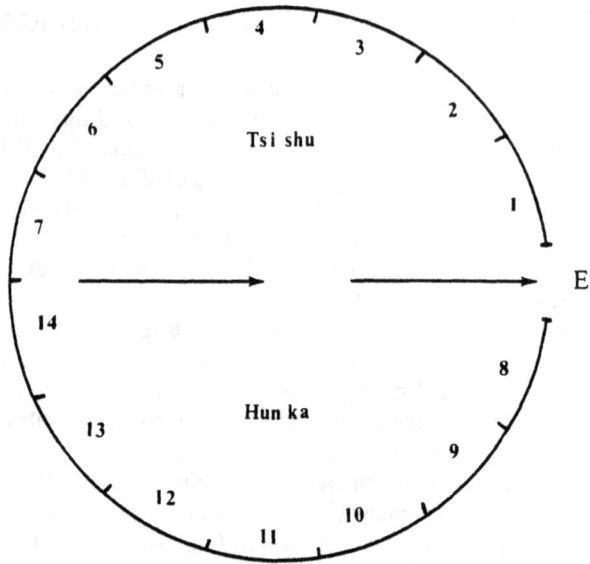

Tribal Circle–Symbolic Order
Fig. 1

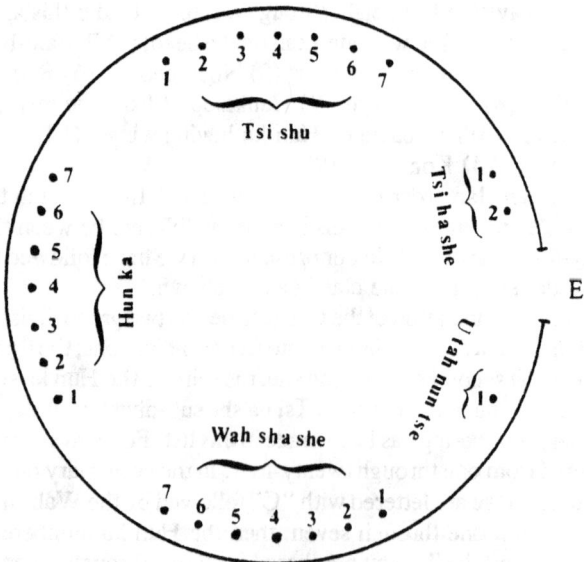

Tribal Circle–Normal Order
Fig. 2

30

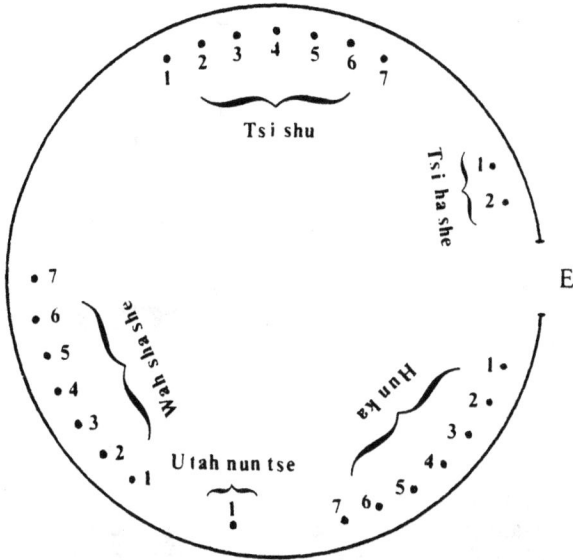

Tribal Circle–Sacred Order
Fig. 3

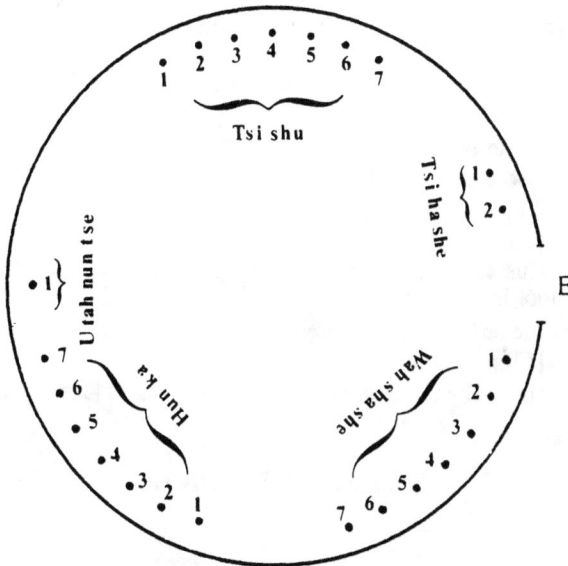

Tribal Circle–Hunting Order
Fig. 4

31

The divisions, sub-divisions, clans, sub-clans and sub-sub-clans are as follows:

HUN KA GRAND DIVISION

CLANS 1-8

THREE SUB-DIVISIONS

Special Sub-Division "C"

One Clan

1. Hun ka u tah nun tse
   [The Isolated Hun ka or Isolated Earth]
   This clan symbolizes the earth in its entirety, and the name expresses the tribal belief that the earth is isolated from the other cosmic bodies.
   It was the keeper of the house wherein the children of all the people were initiated into the tribal life and given their gentile personal name. At times the clan is spoken of as, Instructor of Rites. The ancestors of its members are said to have used the four winds as weapons.
   Two of its life symbols are the spider and the great butterfly.

Three sub-clans

   a. U tah nun tse
      [Isolated Earth People Proper]
   b. Tsa ho pa
      [Spider]
      This sub-clan is placed here by conjecture since the clan's life symbol is the spider.
   c. Moh he se
      [Flint-Arrow Point]
      This sub-clan acts as Sho kah [Messenger] for the clan.

Wah sha she Sub-Division

Seven Clans

2-8

Wah sha she is an archaic name and its true meaning has been lost. La Flesche expressed the thought that the true meaning was probably, name giver.

2. Wah sha she wah nun
   [Elder Osage]

   also

   Ne scah
   [White Water]

   also

   Wah sha rah scah
   [White Osage]
   This refers to the clan's life symbol, the fresh water mussel, with its shell.
   The Nun ne o pah shin ka [Little Pipe] which is a symbolic ceremonial pipe, belongs to this clan.

   Two sub-clans

   a. U kon scah
      [The Middle People]
      It should be noted here that the true name of the Osage people is Ne U kon scah [People of the Middle Waters].
   b. E glo gah ne moh tsa
      [Puma in the Water]
      This sub-clan is Sho kah [Messenger] for its clan.
3. Ka ke en
   [Carrier of the Turtle]

   Four sub-clans

   a. Ke sin tse kah tsa
      [Turtle People]
   b. Tah kon tah
      [Deer Lights]
   c. Wah ha rah stet sy
      [Tall Flags]
   d. Pah ka ah sho e gah rah
      [Cotton-Tree People]
      The cotton-tree symbolized the joining of sky and earth.
4. Me ka rah stet sy
   [Cat-Tail]
   This clan furnishes the third or inner covering for the ceremonial shrine, Wah ho pa. This is a woven-rush bag adorned with the symbols of

the sky and earth. The woof is made of spike rush; the warp is made of nettle weed.

One sub-clan

Kah he wah hu sah
   [Youngest Brother or Loud-Voiced Crow]
   This sub-clan acts as Sho kah [Messenger] for its clan.
5. Pun ka sah sha ta kah
   [Ponca Peacemaker]

also

Wah tsa tse
   [Star that Came to Earth]
   It has been said that a comet fell from the morning star and came to join the council of this clan.
   Hon tsa (shu tsy) [Red Cedar] is the life symbol of this clan.

Five sub-clans

a. Hon tse shu tsy
      [Red Cedar]
b. Warrior Come Hither After Touching the Foe
c. Wah ha la
      [Flags or Standards]
d. Wah tsa tse wah sha ta kah
      [Star Peace]
e. Hu lah pa son sho en gah rah
      [The Bald Eagle People]
      This sub-clan acts as Sho kah [Messenger] for its clan.
6. O su kah ha
   [They Who Make the Way Clear]
   Osage myth relates that this clan led the way when the people descended to earth and searched for the Isolated Earth People. Members of this clan acted as scouts for the war parties.

One sub-clan

Moh sho tsa moie
      [Travelers in the Mist]
      This sub-clan was called upon to cause a fog, or wind to raise the dust, in order to conceal the movements of a war party.
      Sho kah [Messenger] for its clan.

7. Tah lah he
   [Deer Lungs]

also

Tah sen tsa scah
   [White-Tailed Deer]
   This clan furnished the second covering for the ceremonial shrine,
Wah ho pa. The second or middle bag was made of deerskin.

Two sub-clans

a. Tah e ne ka shin ka
   [Little Male Deer]
b. Wah tsu tah shin ka
   [Small Animals]
   Acts as Sho kah [Messenger] for its clan.
8. Ho e ne kah she
   [Fish People]

also

Ka tse u
   [Turtle with Serrated Tail]
   The otter and beaver are life symbols of this clan.

One sub-clan

A nom me tsa to
   [Sole Owner of the Bow]
   This sub-clan holds the office of making the ceremonial bow
and arrows that symbolize night and day.
   The bow is its life symbol.

Hun ka Sub-Division

Seven Clans

9-15

9. Wah sop pe to
   [Owners of the Black Bear]

also

Wah tse ka wa
   [The Radiant Star]
   This clan and the Puma clan kept the house where war ceremonies
were held. Both clans also shared the swallow as a life symbol.

Four sub-sub-clans

a. Lah ke to pah sin tse he
   [Wearing Four Locks of Hair]
   (1) Me hah scah
      [Swan]
   (2) Me ta pa ne to op pe pe se
      [Dried Pond Lily]
b. Sin tse e gah heh
   [Wearing a Tail of Hair on the Head]
   (1) Wah sop pe
      [Black Bear]
   (2) Wah sop pe scah
      [White Bear]
      This sub-sub-clan acts as Sho kah [Messenger] for its clan.

10. E gro ka
    [Puma]
    This clan and the Owners of the Black Bear clan kept the house where war ceremonies were held. Both clans also share the swallow as a life symbol.

Two sub-clans

a. E gro ka
   [Puma People Proper]
b. Hu wah hah gah
   [Thorny Hair – Porcupine]
   This sub-clan acts as Sho kah [Messenger] for its clan.

11. O pon
    [Elk]
    The elk was called black breast and big earth maker. He splashed up huge waves creating the dry land of the earth.

Two sub-clans

a. O pon
   [Elk People Proper]
b. Tah he sop pe
   [Dark Horned Deer]
   This sub-clan acts as Sho kah [Messenger] for its clan.

12. Moh e kah gah he
    [Maker of the Earth]
    In one myth the Elk made the earth and is called the Big Earth Maker;
    in another the Crawfish dove into the waters and brought four colors of
    earth up in his claws. The Crawfish is called the Little Earth Maker.

                        One sub-clan

    Moh se kon
    [Crawfish]
                          also
    Hun ka shin ka
    [Little Earth]
13. Hun ka grah she
    [The Mottled Sacred One] [Mottled Eagle]
    This refers to the immature golden eagle called the stainless one.

                     No known sub-clans

14. Hu lah
    [Eagle]
    This refers to the adult golden eagle.
    The life symbol of this clan is the dark-plumed golden eagle.

                        Two sub-clans

    a. He sah to
       [Outstretched Leg or Leg Outstretched]
       This refers to the eagle leg attached to the Wa ho pa, [ceremonial
       shrine].
    b. Hun ka ah hu tun
       [Hun ka Having Wings]
15. Hun ka shin ka
    [The Little Sacred One]
                          also
    Hun ka u lum ha ka
    [Last in the Hun ka Order]
                          also
    E pa tsa ta tsa
    [The Four Winds]
    Dorsey gives this clan as Kan sa but La Flesche states this is an error
    of confusion arising from the Omaha name for this clan. Dorsey places the

Winds sub-clan in this clan while La Flesche places it in the Elk clan. From the name Hun ka, popular in the Winds sub-clan, it would seem to belong here. Alice C. Fletcher does not mention the Winds clan or sub-clan. Certainly a close relationship exists between the Wind and Elk clans, but we are following Dorsey's earlier placement.

The office of herald was vested in this clan. It also lights the ceremonial pipes and conducts the spirit ceremonies.

Three sub-clans

a. E pa tse
   [Pipe Lighter]
b. E pa tsa
   [Wind]
c. E pa tse tah tsa
   [The Gathering of the Winds]
   Acts as Sho ka [Messenger] for its clan.

TSI SHU GRAND DIVISION

CLANS 16-24

TWO SUB-DIVISIONS

Tsi shu Sub-Division

Seven Clans

16. Tsi shu wah nun
    [Elder Tsi shu]

also

Wa kon ta nun pa pe
[The God Who is Feared By All] [Sun People]
   This refers to one of the clan's life symbols, the sun. Other life symbols are Wah shin ka stet sy tsa [Long-Billed Bird — Pileated Woodpecker] and Pe shu sha ka [The Night-Hawk].

Two sub-clans

a. Tsa to hah
   [Hide with the Hair On]

b. Wah pa he
  [The Awakeners]
  This refers to the sub-clan's office of urging the messengers to prompt action.
  Acts as Sho kah [Messenger] for its clan.
17. Sen tsa ah grah
  [Wearers of Symbolic Locks]
  Members of this clan wore a wolf tail on the scalp lock.

Two sub-clans

a. Shon ka sho e kah rah
  [Wolf People]
b. Me ka kah shon ka e kah rah
  [Dog Star People]
  This refers to the life symbol of this sub-clan, the dog star.
  Acts as Sho kah [Messenger] for its clan.
18. Pa to tun ka sho in ka rah
  [Great Crane People]

No known sub-clans

19. Tsa to kah in tsa
  [Buffalo Bull Face]
  This clan is said to be closely related to the Elder Tsi shu.
  It has been said that Wah pa he went in search of game. He found a buffalo, pointed his finger at its face and killed it; Wah kon ta reproved him for the act. Because of this deed his people were called Buffalo Bull Face People.

One sub-clan

Tsa ah ko
  [Buffalo Back]
  Tsa ah ko is supposed to be a corruption of Tsa lum ka [Buffalo Back].
  Acts as Sho kah [Messenger] for its clan.
20. Tsi shu wah sha ta kah
  [Gentle Tsi shu or Dawn People]
  This refers to the clan's office of peacemaker.
                        also
Me ka in wah nun
  [Elder Carriers of the Sun and Moon or Elder Sun Carriers]

39

This refers to one set of the clan's life symbols, all the heavenly bodies. Another life symbol is Tsa pe la tun ka [Great Dragon-Fly].

Five sub-clans plus
Four sub-clans placed by conjecture
One sub-sub-clan

a. Tse u kon scah
   [House in the Center]
   The Tsi shu chief was taken from this clan. His house was located in the center of the village opposite the Hun ka chief's house.
b. Bah po
   [Elderberry Bush]
   The stem of ceremonial pipes were made of elderberry. The boys made poppers from the branches of the elderberry, hence the name bah po from the popping sound.
c. Moh sah he
   [Arrow Tree]
d. Shon son he
   [Sycamore Tree]
e. Tse u lu ha ka
   [Last Group of Houses]
                        also
   He la sha [possibly shu tsy]
   [Red Eagle]
   This is actually a red-tailed hawk.
   Acts as Sho kah [Messenger] for its clan.

One sub-sub-clan

Hun pa log ny
[Peaceful Days]
The following are placed here by conjecture. They may be sub-sub-clans or they may belong to some other clan. Another possibility is, they may be alternate names for the sub-clans above or additional sub-clans. In any event, they seem to belong with this clan.
   (f) Me o pah
       [Moon]
   (g) Me ka kah
       [Star]
   (h) Me ka kah sin tse stet sy
       [Sun and Comet]

    (i) Wah pah e tah she
        [Those Who Do Not Touch Blood]
21. Hon e ne ka she
    [Night People]
    This refers to the clan's life symbol, the night.

Four sub-clans

a. Hon e ne ka she ka
    [Night People Proper]
b. Wah sop pe [possibly shu tsy]
    [Red Bear]
c. Pa tsa
    [Fire]
d. Tah pah sho e ka rah
    [Deer Head – Peleides People]
    Acts as Sho kah [Messenger] for its clan.
22. Tsi shu u thu hah ka
    [The Last Tsi shu]
    This indicates the clan was last in the sequential order of the Tsi shu.

No known sub-clans

Tsi Ha She Sub-Division

Two Clans

"A" "B"

23-24

Tsi ha she means those who were last to come. This indicates they were the last to become a part of the Osage tribe. These two clans are not normally numbered but are designated "A" and "B". The same is true of clan one in this list, which normally is designated as clan "C".
23. Ne kah wah kon tah ke
    [Men of Mystery]
also
Glo e
[Thunder Being]
    This clan and the Buffalo Bull clan are joint keepers of the hawk Wa ho pa.
    The life symbol of this clan is, Gla to [Hawk].

41

Five sub-clans

a. Glo e ne ka she kah
   [Thunder People Proper]
b. Nu ha
   [Ice]
   This refers to ice or hail associated with thunder storms.
c. To won glo
   [Thunder Town]
d. Ho tse wah tse
   [Cedar Star]
e. Hun tsa wah tsa
   [To Touch Cedar]
   This refers to striking an enemy. Thunder rested on the top of the cedars as it descended.
   Acts as Sho kah [Messenger] for its clan.

24. Lo ha
   [Buffalo Bull]
   This is said to be an archaic name for Tsa to kah [Buffalo Bull].

This clan and the Men of Mystery clan are the joint keepers of the hawk war symbols and are said to have introduced it as the Wa ho pa. It is this clan that furnishes the woven buffalo hair bag to cover the ceremonial shrine, Wa ho pa. This constitutes the first or outer covering.

The life symbols of the clan are Gla to [Hawk], Ha pa [Corn], Tsa [Buffalo] and Ne sha ku the [Bank Swallow].

Two sub-clans

a. Tsa to kah
   [Buffalo Bull People Proper]
b. To kah shu tsy sop pe
   [Reddish Bull]

OSAGE PERSONAL NAMES

Naming an Osage child was an important tribal event. No respectable Osage family neglected to have their children named in the child naming ceremony. Child naming was not a mere matter of vanity or fashion; it was a part of the fabric of tribal organization.

Tribal organization rests on the ties within the families of its members. Families were members of groups of related families called clans. Related clans formed sub-divisions and related sub-divisions formed divisions. Union of divisions created the tribe. For biological reasons and to promote inter-clan ties a person could not marry within their clan. In fact, marriages within the sub-division were discouraged by the Osages. Child naming was the individual's introduction and acceptance into this gentile system. Without having a name, ceremonially bestowed, an individual was a nobody or non-person in the gentile organization. That is, they were not members of the tribe, since they could not participate in tribal ceremonies, and in this sense they were outcasts. They were of the blood but not of the tribe.

Only the first three sons and the first three daughters were named in a child naming ceremony. Subsequent children were considered to be ceremonially named if the first three sons and first three daughters had been ceremonially named. The first three sons and the first three daughters each had special kinship terms by which they were addressed only by close family members. These terms were not used outside the family, since they were not personal names. In the child naming ceremony, the child was given a traditional personal name of the clan reserved for the first son, etc. or the first daughter, etc.

These traditional personal names of the clans are as near to a surname, common in Western Civilization, as one can find among the traditional Osages. Osage surnames came into use as the influence of Western Civilization grew. Surnames as a concept in naming, were alien to the Osage culture. The clan was every Osage's father, therefore, the names were clan names.

Clan names, ceremonially bestowed, met two conditions. First, the name was reserved specifically for the first born, second born, etc. within the specific clan. Although some of these names were used by more than one clan, in the main, they are indicative of a specific clan. A second condition is, the ceremonial name must relate to a legendary event. Some of these names are sky names and others are earth names. Sky names are those associated with legendary events which occurred before the people descended to earth. Earth names relate to legendary events which occurred after the people descended to earth.

For many of the Osage people, especially the women, these were the only

43

names they used in their entire lives. Some, especially the men, adopted another name in later life. Usually these adopted names were also clan or gentile names. Yet, there were several types of adopted names, two classes of adopted names followed the gentile naming custom.

One class of adopted names were taken from the legends and were strictly clan names. While these names were almost universally earth names, a few were sky names. Ha pa shu tsy or Red Corn is an adopted name of this class. Another adopted name of this type but in a different class, is the clan office names. All these names refer to some office or function the clan performs within the gentile organization. Soldier or Protector names are typical of this class. The ceremonial names, adopted clan names and office names are all ne ke a or gentile names.

Other adopted names fall within three types. These are honor names, war names and personal choice names. None of these names are ne ke a. The women use an honor name which is Ki he ka wa ko or Woman Chief. Black Dog was given the honor name of Man Ka shon ka or Cut With Axe Dog, because he built the Black Dog Trail. Che to pa or Four Lodges is a war name, whichs refers to the destruction of four enemy lodges. War names are, naturally, common among the men.

Originally, personal choice names were not common in the tribe and they varied greatly in characteristics. Ka wa se or Yellow Horse is a typical personal choice name. The horse names are non ne ke a adopted names. A new class of personal choice names enter the Osage naming practices as contact with Western Civilization increased.

At first, contact with Western Civilization had little impact on Osage names. Osage vocabulary experienced almost immediate rapid growth, but names seemed to resist the exposure to the new culture. Gradually names were altered through errors in both phonics and translation. Thus, we find Gra moie altered to Claremore and Wa sha she to Osage. Many times these names were filtered through both French and English language errors. Another source of name changes came from the European practice of using translated names until the Osage person adopted the translated name. Pa hu scah adopted the White Hair name first in the French translation, Cheveux Blanc and then in the English translation, White Hair.

As more and more Osage children attended schools of the Western Civilization, their names suffered great changes. Teachers either could not or would not use Osage names. To avoid using Osage names, they gave Osage pupils names from the textbooks. In this way, names such as William Penn began to appear as an Osage name. Earlier, it had been customary to give an Osage a first name in English and retain the father's name in Osage. This arose from the baptisms performed by the Jesuits. The Jesuits recorded the baptism under the father's name and the baptismal name of the child. In this way, such names as Louis Me ti an ka and Mary Mo shon kah she became commonplace.

It is interesting to note, this is one of the few naming practices of this class, that preserves the Osage names. However, it does this by using the surname practices of Western Civilization.

Before we turn to the list of Osage names, we must also be aware that many Osage families have adopted English surnames. In the predominant culture, it is convenient to have an English name and to follow English cultural practice in naming. This is not a matter of "turning the back" to Osage culture. It is a means of solving the problem of ignorance and indifference in the predominant culture toward Osage culture. The great danger in this practice lies in the tendency to "throw away" the Osage naming practices and in the process losing a vital part of Osage culture. Adopting and using English naming practices should not prevent an Osage from also following Osage naming practices.

EXPLANATIONS FOR THE LIST
OF OSAGE NAMES BY CLAN

The list of Osage names following this explanation needs a few comments. Each set of names are arranged under their respective clans. All but a few of the names are ne ke a or gentile names, except as otherwise noted. Often the spouse or parent is also given and some include the spouse's clan. For most of the clans, the special kinship terms and names for the first three sons and the first three daughters are also given.

This list was compiled by Dr. Francis La Flesche in the early 1900's. It was published in the Smithsonian Institution, Bureau of Ethnology, Forty-third Annual Report, 1925-1926, pp. 124-165. We have copied this list with only three changes. First, we have changed the phonics to English phonics and translated the clan names into English. Next, we omitted distracting material; this was mainly comparisons with the Omaha tribe, which had no bearing on our purposes. Finally, we added pertinent information. This information is enclosed in brackets[] so the reader can account for the source. We also numbered the entries for reference purposes. Material enclosed in parentheses () was placed in parentheses by Dr. La Flesche. La Flesche apparently did not offer any speculative translations, nor did we. All the translations are positive and have been well verified. Rather than offer a speculative translation, Dr. La Flesche indicated, meaning uncertain or meaning obscure. In a few cases the translation was omitted without comment. .

Dr. La Flesche was not clear in his use of the term Hun ka clan. Since there were seven Hun ka clans, a doubt arises about which of the seven clans he means when he uses the term Hun ka clan. The third name in the Hun ka u lum ha ka, Last in the Hun ka Order clan tells us this is the clan he means, when he writes a person is of the Hun ka clan.

Another problem arises from the phonics. In English phonics La Flesche's ho^n may be ho, hum or hun. In his phonics, he also has ho which is the same as ho in English. The problem arises because two clans have similar names. Ho e ne ka she ka, Fish People, and Hun e ne ka she ka, Night People, are easily confused unless one carefully notes La Flesche's distinction between ho, fish and ho^n, night, when changing to English phonics. Although we double checked all reference to these two clans we still urge caution where these clans are concerned.

LIST OF OSAGE NAMES BY CLAN

Clan A

WA TSA TSE or PON KA WA ESTAH

[Ponca Peace Maker]

Names ceremonially bestowed on each of the first three sons and on each of the first three daughters born to a Pon ka Peace Maker man and his wife. These were given by Non he scah she, a member of the clan.

Sons

1st. E gra name, Wa se se ta, meaning uncertain.
2nd. K shon ka name, Wa tsa moie, Star That Travels.
3rd. Ka shin ka name, Ne ka to he, Water Splasher.

Daughters

1st. Me na name, Hum pa to ka, Wet Moccasins.
2nd. We ha name, Wa to e sa a, meaning uncertain, also Me ka shon a, Sun That Travels.
3rd. Ah se ka name, Kea sum pa, meaning uncertain.

OTHER NAMES

Male

1. Gra e gro le ke, meaning uncertain. Son of Lum tse tun ka and Hu lah to me of the Tsi shu Peace Maker clan.
2. Gra to wa kon la, Attacking Hawk (Buffalo Bull clan name). Son of Tsi shu a ke pa and Hum pa to ka of the Little Male Deer clan.
3. He lo ka le, Bare Legs also Ku she wa tsa, Strikes in a Far Off Country.
4. He lo ka le or Long Bow. [Perhaps this should be Me tsa stah tsy or Me tsa stet sy.]
5. Hu lah tse, Real Eagle. Husband of Wa ko ki he ka of the Tsi shu Peace Maker clan.
6. Ka scah, meaning uncertain. Son of Pon ka shin ka and Hu lah to me of the Tsi shu Peace Maker clan.
7. Ka scah. Son of Lum tse tun ka and Hu lah to me of the Tsi shu Peace Maker clan.

8. Ka se, meaning uncertain.
9. Ke le kon pe, One For Whom They Make Way. Husband of Moh se tsa he of the Tsi shu Peace Maker clan.
10. Ko she se gra, Tracks Far Away. Husband of Hu lah to me of the Tsi shu Peace Maker clan.
11. Ko she se gra, Husband of Shon bla scah me of the Isolated Earth clan.
12. K shon ka. This is not a name but a special kinship term for the second born son. The name should be Ah pa shin ka, Slender Leaf, of the cattail.
13. Lo tsa tun ka, Big Heart. Also Wa shin wa ha, Greatest in Courage. Husband of Hu lah to me of the Tsi shu Peace Maker clan.
14. Pon ka wa ti an ka, Playful Pon ka. [Sometimes Saucy Pon ka.] Husband of Wa ke lo pa of the Elder Tsi shu clan.
15. Tsi shu ah ke pa, He Who Met the Tsi shu. Husband of Hum pa to ka of the Little Male Deer clan.
16. Tsi shu ah ke pa. Husband of Wa ke lo pa of the Elder Tsi shu clan.
17. U lo ka a, meaning uncertain. (Not a Ne Ke a name.)
18. U tsa ta wa ha, Winner Of The Race Against The U tsa ta. (Not a Ne ke a name.)
19. Wa ha ka tsa, meaning uncertain. Husband of No me tsa he of the Black Bear clan.
20. Wa se se ta, meaning uncertain. Son of Pon ka wa ti an ka and Wa ke lo ha of the Elder Tsi shu clan.
21. Wa se se ta. Son of Wa ha ka tsa and No me tsa he of the Black Bear clan.
22. Wa shin wa ha, Greatest In Courage. Husband of Moh shon tsa ta of the Tsi shu Peace Maker clan.
23. Wa shin wa ha. Son of Moh kon ah le.
24. Wa stat a to, Good Doctor. [This is written Wah stah to a in the Annuity Rolls.] (Some say the boy's right name is Wa tsa moie.) Son of Pon ka wa ti an ka and Wa ke lo pa of the Elder Tsi shu clan.
25. Wa tse ah ha, Cries For A Star. Son of U lo ka a.
26. Wa tse ki he ka, Star Chief.
27. Wa tse moie, The Traveling Star. Husband of Wa kon sa moie of the Little Male Deer clan.
28. Wa tse moie. Son of Wa ko ki he ka of the Elder Tsi shu clan.
29. Wa tse moie. Son of Ka she se gra and Hu lah to me of the Elder Tsi shu clan.
30. Wa tse moie. Son of He lo ka le. (Long Bow.) [This name, Long Bow, is written Me tsa stah tsy and Me tsa stet sy in the Annuity Rolls.]
31. Wa tse tun ka, Big Star.

Female

1. Hu lah to me, Good Eagle Woman. Daughter of Tsi shu ah ke pa and Hum pa to ka of the Little Male Deer clan.
2. Hum pa to ka, Wet Moccasins. Daughter of Wa shin wa ha and Moh shon tse e ta of the Tsi shu Peace Maker clan.
3. Hum pa to ka. Daughter of U lo ka a.
4. Hum pa to ka. Daughter of Tsi shu ah ke pa and Wa ke lo pa of the Elder Tsi shu clan.
5. Hum pa to ka. Mother of Hu lah wa kon ta, Kea sum pa and Hu lah to me of the Elder Tsi shu clan.
6. Hum pa to ka. Daughter of Moh kon ah le.
7. Hum pa to ka. Wife of Moh shon ah ke ta of the Tsi shu Peace Maker clan.
8. Hum pa to ka. Wife of Ha he u me she of the Tsi shu Peace Maker clan.
9. Hum pa to ka. Daughter of Wa tsa ah he and Pa moh she wa glo of the Elk clan.
10. Hum pa to ka. Daughter of Ko she se gra and Hu lah to me of the Tsi shu Peace Maker clan.
11. Hum pa to ka. Daughter of Wa ha ka tsa and No me tsa he of the Black Bear clan.
12. Kea sum pa, meaning uncertain. Wife of U hun ka u shon of the Wearers Of The Symbolic Locks clan.
13. Kea sum pa. Wife of Ka wa se of the Wind clan.
14. Kea sum pa. Daughter of Tsi shu ah ke pa and Wa ke lo pa of the Elder Tsi shu clan.
15. Kea sum pa. Mother of Me hun ka, Hu lah wa kon ta and Sha ke wa pe of the Elder Tsi shu clan.
16. Kea sum pa. Daughter of Ko she se gra and Hu lah to me of the Tsi shu Peace Maker clan.
17. Kea sum pa. Daughter of Wa ha ka tsa and No me tse he.
18. Kea sum pa. Wife of Lo ha shin ka of the Buffalo Bull clan.
19. Me ka shon e, Sun That Travels. Daughter of Pon ka wa ti an ka and Wa ke lo pa of the Elder Tsi shu clan.
20. Me ka shon e. Wife of Moh shin scah ke ka hre of the Black Bear clan.
21. Me ka shon e. Wife of Gra to scah of the Men of Mystery clan.
22. Me log ny, Good Sun. Daughter of Moh e ka moie and Hu lah to me of the Wearers Of Symbolic Locks clan.
23. Pon ka me, Pon ka Woman. (This woman held the office of Wa tsa pa en, Official Crier.)
24. Son se gra, Footprints In The Woods. Wife of Hum pa hu of the Little Male Deer clan.
25. Wa kon sa moie, meaning uncertain. Daughter of U lo ka a.

26. Wa kon sa moie. Mother of Lo ta ah sa, Ho ta me and Hun tsa moie of the Men Of Mystery clan.
27. Wa kon sa moie. Wife of Tsa sa tun ka of the Buffalo Bull clan.
28. Wa Kon sa moie. Daughter of Wa ko ki he ka of the Tsi Peace Maker clan.
29. Wa kon sa moie. Wife of Me she tse a of the Hun ka clan.
30. Wa kon sa moie. Wife of Wa ne a tun of the Tsi shu Peace Maker clan.
31. Wa kon sa moie. Daughter of Wa tsa ah ha and Pa moh she wa glo.
32. Wa kon sa moie. Daughter of Ko she se gra and Hu lah to me.
33. Wa kon sa moie. Daughter of Lo tsa tun ka and Hu lah to me.
34. Wa kon sa moie. Daughter of Wa ha ka tsa and No me tsa he.
35. Wa to e sa, meaning uncertain. Wife of Moh ka ha of the Puma or Panther clan.
36. Wa to e sa. Wife of O pah lo a of the Tsi shu Peace Maker clan.
37. Wa to e sa. Wife of A to moie of the Sun Carrier clan.
38. Wa to e sa. Daughter of Pon ka wa ti an ka and Wa ke lo pa.
39. Wa to e sa. Wife of No po a of the Isolated Earth clan.
40. Wa to e sa. Daughter of Wa tsa ki he ka.
41. Wa to e sa. Wife of Kah wa hoi tsa of the Wind clan.
42. Wa to e sa. Daughter of Wa ha ka tsa and No me tsa he.
43. We ha. This is not a name but a special kinship term for the second daughter in a family. Daughter of Wa tsa ki he ka.

Clan B

TAH E NE KA SHIN KA

[Little Male Deer]

Special kinship terms and names of the first three sons and the first three daughters in a family of the Little Male Deer clan, as given by Tish she walla, a member of the clan.

Sons

1st. E gra name, Wa sha she hun ka, Sacred Wa sha she.
2nd. K shon ka name, To ho ho a, Blue Fish.
3rd. Ka shin ka name, Ho ke ah se, Wriggling Fish.

Daughters

1st. Me na name, Wa sha she me tsa he, Wa sha she Sacred Sun.
2nd. We ha name, Hum pa to ka, Wet Moccasins.
3rd. Se ka name, Shon se gra, Footprints In The Woods.

OTHER NAMES

Male

1. Ah ke ta shin ka, Little Soldier. [Sometimes given as Little Protector.] Husband of Hu lah to me of the Tsi shu Peace Maker clan.
2. A nom me tsa to, Sole Owner of the Bow. Son of To ho ho a. [Sole Owner of the Bow is the name of a sub-clan of the Fish People clan.]
3. A nom me tsa to. Son of Ho ke a se and Me tsa he of the Hun ka clan.
4. A nom me tsa to. Son of Tah ha ka ha and Wa hu ka he of the Wind clan.
5. Che she walla, Rustles The Leaves. Husband of Ne Ka she tse a of the Night People clan.
6. Ho ho, Fish Scales. Son of Me tsa he of the Hun ka clan.
7. Ho ho a, Fish Scales. Son of To ho ho a.
8. Ho ke ah se, Wriggling Fish. Son of To ho ho a.
9. Ho ke ah se. Son of Ta he ha he and Wa hu son a of the Wind clan.
10. Ho ke ah se, also Ko she moie, Wanders Far Away. Husband of Me tsa he of the Hun ka clan.
11. Ho son, White Fish. Son of Ah ka me of the Wind clan.

51

12. Ki he ka nah she, Standing Chief. Husband of Hu lah to me of the Tsi shu Peace Maker clan.
13. Ki he ka log ny, Good Chief. Son of Me tsa he of the Night People clan.
14. Ki he ka shin ka, Young Chief. [The name is sometimes given as Little Chief.]
15. Le he pe, Scared Up. Husband of Me tsa he of the Night People clan.
16. Moh ke ha pe, For Whom Arrows Are Made. Son of Ki he ka no shin and Hu lah to me of the Tsi shu Peace Maker clan.
17. No she walla, Causes Them To Stand. Father of Wa sha she me tsa he.
18. O ho pe, One Who Is Cooked. Son of To pa pe of the Isolated Earth clan.
19. Son tsa kon ha, Edge Of The Forest. Husband of Hu lah to me of the Tsi shu Peace Maker clan.
20. Tah se a, Deer Tail.
21. Tah ha ka he, Deer With Branching Horns. Husband of Wa hu son a of the Wind clan.
22. Tah she ka, Deer's Leg.
23. To ho ho a, Blue Fish.
24. To ho ho a. Son of Ho ke a se and Me tsa he of the Isolated Earth clan.
25. Tsa to ha, Buffalo Hide (a Buffalo Bull name); also Wa sha no pa en, meaning uncertain.
26. Wa kon tse a, One Who Wins Triumphs. Husband of He e ke op pe of the Tsi shu Peace Maker clan.
27. Wa sha a no pa en, meaning uncertain. Son of Tah she ka.
28. Wa sha a no pa en. Son of Me tsa he of the Hun ka clan.
29. Wa sha hun ka, Sacred Wa sha she. Son of To ho ho a.
30. Wa sha hun ka. Husband of Me gra to me.
31. Wa sha hun ka. Son of Wa sha hun ka and Me gra to me.
32. Wa sha she, meaning uncertain. Son of Me tsa he of the Isolated Earth clan.

Female

1. Gra to me shin ka, Young Hawk Woman. [Sometimes given as Little Hawk Woman.] Wife of Ke wa hre she of the Isolated Earth clan.
2. Hum pa to ka, Wet Moccasins. Wife of Tsi shu ah ke pa of the Pon ka Peace Maker clan.
3. Hum pa to ka. Wife of A gra ka shin ka of the Black Bear clan.
4. Hum pa to ka. Wife of We tun ha e ka of the Men of Mystery clan.
5. Hum pa to ka. Daughter of Ki he ka no shin and Hu lah to me of the Tsi shu Peace Maker clan.
6. Hum pa to ka. Wife of Hum pa hu of the Night People clan.
7. Hum pa to ka. Daughter of To ho ho a.

8. Ne op pe, Permitted To Live.
9. Ne to pa, Sees Water. Daughter of To ho ho a.
10. Pa ha pe son tsa, Stunted Oaks.
11. Pa ha pe son tsa. Wife of Hu lah tun ka of the Hun ka clan.
12. Pa ha pe son tsa. Wife of Tsa sen tsa of the Buffalo Bull clan.
13. Pa ha pe son tsa. Wife of To le hre hro tsa of the Tsi shu Peace Maker clan.
14. Pa hu gra sa, Spotted Hair. Mother of Andrew O pah of the Elk clan.
15. Son se gra, Footprints In The Woods. Wife of To won ka he of the Tsi shu Peace Maker clan.
16. Son se gra. Wife of Tsa wa hu of the Elder Tsi shu clan.
17. Son se gra. Daughter of Che she walla and Ne ka she tse.
18. Wa kon sa moie, meaning uncertain. Wife of Wa tsa moie.
19. Wa sha she me tsa he, Wa sha she Sacred Sun. Daughter of No she walla.
20. Wa sha she me tsa he. Wife of Pa seo tun ka, a Kaw Indian.
21. Wa sha she me tsa he. Wife of No pa se of the Tsi shu Peace Maker clan.
22. Wa sha she me tsa he. Daughter of Wa ko tse a and He e ke ta pe of the Tsi shu Peace Maker clan.
23. Wa sha she me tsa he. Daughter of Che she walla and Ne ka she tsa a of the Fish People clan.
24. Wa sha she me tsa he. Daughter of Ki he ka no shin and Hu lah to me of the Tsi shu Peace Maker clan.
25. Wa sha she me tsa he. Daughter of Me tsa he of the Hun ka clan.
26. Wa to e sa a, meaning uncertain. Wife of Moh ka sho a of the Buffalo Bull clan.

Clan C

HO E NE KA SHE KA

[Fish People]

Special kinship terms and names of the first three sons and first three daughters in a family of the Fish People clan.

Sons

1st. E gra name, Wa sha hun ka, Sacred Wa sha she.
2nd. K shon ka name, To ho ho, Blue Fish.
3rd. Ka shin ka name, Ho Ho a, Fish Scales.

Daughters

1st. Me na name, Wa sha she me tsa he, Wa sha she Sacred Sun.
2nd. We ha name, Hum pa to ka, Wet Moccasins.
3rd. Se ka name, Wa sha me tsa he, Sacred Sun.

OTHER NAMES

Male

1. A nom me tsa to, Sole Owner Of The Bow. [This is the name of a sub-clan which belongs to the Fish People clan.]
2. Che she walla, Rustles The Leaves.
3. E stah pa tsa, Fire Eyes.
4. He scah moie, White Horn Walks.
5. Ho bla scah shin ka, Little Flat Fish.
6. Ho he ha, Fish Skin.
7. Ho ka ha, Fish Fins.
8. Ho ke a se, Splashing Fish.
9. Ho pa, Fish Head.
10. Ho scah, White Fish.
11. Ho son, Braided Fish.
12. Ho wa he, Fish Bone.
13. Ki he ka no shin, Standing Chief.
14. Ki he ka log ny, Handsome Chief. [Sometimes given as Good Chief.]
15. Ki he ka tun ka, Big Chief.

16. Ki he ka shin ka, Little Chief.
17. Ki he ka ha tse, Real Chief.
18. Ko she moie, Travels In Distant Lands.
19. Me ka ha ka, Crying Coon.
20. Men tsa ne a, Fences With The Bow.
21. Ne u pa shu tsy, Muddies The Waters.
22. Tah ha ka ha, Antlered Deer.
23. Tah ha ha ka, Rough Horned Deer.
24. Tsa to ha, Buffalo Skin. (A name belonging to the Buffalo Bull clan.)

Female

1. Me gra to me, Hawk Woman.
2. Nom ka scah, White Back.
3. Nom tah scah, White Ears.
4. Pa hop pe son tsa, Frequenter Of Bushes.
5. Pa hu gra she, Spotted Hair.
6. Son se gra, Here Are The Footprints. [Sometimes given as Foot Prints In The Forest.]
7. Wa ka lum pa, meaning uncertain.
8. Wa kon se, Small Animal.

Clan D

HUN KA U TA NUM TSE

[Isolated Earth]

Special kinship terms and names of the first three sons and first three daughters in a family of the Isolated Earth clan.

Sons

1st. E gra name, Ta tsa ko a, Soughing Of The Wind.
2nd. K shon name, Ta tsa to, Owners Of The Wind. Also Hun ka u ta nun tse, The Solitary Hun ka.
3rd. Ka shin ka name, Hun ka tse no shin, Standing House Of The Hun ka, also Hun Ka to ka, Great Hun ka; Tse wa kon ta ke, Mystery House; Tse wa le she, Tears Down The House.

Daughters

1st. Me na name, Me tsa he, Me na The Favored.
2nd. We he name, Hu lah to me, Sees The Eagle.
3rd. Se ka name, Me tsa he hun ka, Me na Hun ka The Favored.

OTHER NAMES

Male

1. E ho la pe, From Whom Permission Is Obtained.
2. Hun ka to ka, Great Hunka. Also Ho moh ta ko, Light On Earth At Night. Husband of Pa she he of the Hun ka clan.
3. Hun ka wa ti an ka, Playful Hun ka. [Sometimes given as Saucy Hun ka.]
4. Ke wa hre she, Not Stingy. Husband of Gra to me shin ka of the Little Male Deer clan.
5. Kon sa hun ka, Resembling The Hun ka. Husband of Po keo ta of the Buffalo Bull clan.
6. Moh ha ah gra, Reaches The Sky. Husband of Wa kon ta he lum pa of the Elder Tsi shu clan.
7. Moh he se, Fire. Or Arrow Head.
8. No pa a, Flames At Every Step. Husband of Wa to e sa a of the Pon ka Peace Maker clan.

56

9. Ta tsa ko a, Soughing Of The Wind.
10. Ta tsa to, Owner Of The Wind. Son of Kon sa hun ka and Po keo ta.
11. U pa she a, Counsellor.
12. Wa no pah she, Not Afraid.
13. Wa she u tse, Courageous.

Female

1. Ah hu to pa, Four Wings.
2. Me tsa he hun ka, Me na The Sacred One. Daughter of Kon sa hun ka and Po keo ta.
3. Me tsa he hun ka. Wife of O ke sa of the Tsi shu Peace Maker clan.
4. Me tsa he, Me na The Favorite. Daughter of Hun ka tun ka and Pa she he.
5. Shon bla scah me, Flat Wood Woman. Wife of E stah gra sa of the Black Bear clan.
6. Shon bla scah me. Daughter of Hun ka tun ka and Pa she he.
7. To op pe, Seen By All. Daughter of Kon sa hun ka and Po keo ta of the Buffalo Bull clan.
8. To to pa, Seen From Time To Time. Daughter of Hun ka tun ka and Pa she he of the Hun ka clan.
9. To to pa. Mother of O ho pe of the Little Male Deer clan.
10. Wa tsa me, Star Woman. Daughter of Hun ka tun ka and Pa she he.

HUN KA SUB-DIVISION

Clan E

WA SOP PE

[Black Bear]

Special kinship terms and names of the first three sons and the first three daughters in a family of the Black Bear clan as given by Wa tsa moie.

Sons

1st. E gro name, Shin ka ki he ka, Little Chief.
2nd. K shon ka name, Gra to ho tsa, Gray Hawk.
3rd. Ka ke name, Moh he wa kon ta, Mysterious Knife.

Daughters

1st. Me na name, Me tsa he, Me na The Favorite.
2nd. We ha name, Me ho e, [meaning omitted].
3rd. Se ka or Ah se ka name, Ko pa ka she, Flashing Eyes.

OTHER NAMES

Male

1. E gra ka shin ka, Little Puma. [Often given as Little Panther.] Husband of Hum pa to ka of the Little Male Deer clan.
2. E pa shu tsy, Red Handle.
3. E stah moh sa, Flashing Eyes. Husband of Hu lah to me of the Sun Carrier clan.
4. Moh he shu tsy, Red Knife. Son of Moh she scah ka in ka hre and Me ka shon e.
5. Moh lu ha, Ground Cleared Of Grass. Son of Wa tsa moie and Moh son ho e.
6. Moh she scah ka e ka hre, Slayer Of The Warrior With The White Quiver (war name). Husband of Me ka shon e of the Pon ka Peace Maker clan.
7. Moh shon tse se gra, Tracks On The Prairies.

8. Ne ka wa ti an ka, Playful Man. [Often given as Saucy Man.] Also Moh he wa kon ta, Mysterious Knife.
9. Shin ka ki he ka, Young Chief. [Often given as Little Chief.] Son of E pa shu tsy.
10. Wa tsa ka wa, Radiant Star. Son of Wa tsa moie and Moh son ho e.
11. Wa tsa moie, He Who Wins War Honors (war name). Also Wa she ha. Husband of Me son ho e of the Elk clan.

Female

1. Ko pa ka she, The Light.
2. Ko pa ka she. Daughter of Wa tsa moie and Me son ho e.
3. Me ho e, meaning uncertain. Daughter of E gro ka shin ka and Ho pa to ka.
4. Me ho e. Daughter of Ne ka wa ti an ka.
5. Me ho e. Daughter of Wa tsa moie and Me son ho e.
6. Me son a, White sun. Wife of Wa to e ke la of the Buffalo Bull clan.
7. Me tsa he, Me na The Favorite. Daughter of Moh she scah ka e ka hre and Me ka shon e.
8. No me tsa he, Me na The Favorite. Daughter of Ne ka wa ti an ka.
9. Wa sop pe wa ko, Black Bear Woman. Daughter of E gro ka shin ka.

Clan F

E GRO KA

[Puma or Panther]

Special kinship terms and names of the first three sons and first three daughters in a family of the Puma or Panther clan.

Sons

1st. E gro name, Me wa ka ha, Child Of The Sun.
2nd. K shon ka name, E a scah wa le, Giver Of Speech.
3rd. Ka shin ka name, Moh ka ha, Arrow Maker.

Daughters

1st. Me na name, Moh se tsa he, Sacred Arrow Shaft.
2nd. Me ha name, Moh shon op she me, Woman Who Travels Over The Earth.
3rd. Se ka name, Nah me tsa he, Beloved Child Of The Sun.

OTHER NAMES

Male

1. E stah sop pe, Dark Eyes.
2. Me wa ka ha, Child Of The Sun. Also, He wa ha ka, Rough Hair. Husband of Me tsa he of the Hun ka clan.
3. Moh he wa kon ta, Mysterious Knife. Son of Wa lu tsa ka she and Me tsa he.
4. Moh ka ha, Arrow Maker. Husband of Wa to e sa a of the Pon ka Peace Maker clan. (Also Pa ha ka, Brown Nose.)
5. Moh ka ha. Son of Wa hre she and Hu lah to me.
6. Non pa wa kon ta, Mysterious Hand. Son of Wa lu tsa ka she and Me tsa he.
7. To tsa ah she, meaning obscure.
8. Wa hre she, Generous (war name). Husband of Hu lah to me of the Tsi shu Peace Maker clan.
9. Wa lu tsa ka she, Never Fails (war name). Husband of Me tsa he of the Hun ka clan.

60

Female

1. Me ho e, meaning obscure. Mother of Ho ka of the Men of Mystery clan.
2. Moh se tsa he, Sacred Arrowshaft. Daughter of Wa hre she and Hu lah to me.
3. Moh se tsa he. Mother of E shon pa of the Men of Mystery clan.
4. No me tsa he, Only Sacred Sun. Daughter of Wa hre she and hu lah to me.
5. No me tsa he. Wife of Wa ha ka tsa of the Pon ka Peace Maker clan.
6. Wa tsa me, Star Woman. Wife of He lah u ka shon of the Hun ka clan.

Clan G

HUN KA GRA SHE

[Mottled Eagle]

Special kinship terms and names of the first three sons and the first three daughters in a family of the Mottled Eagle clan, as given by Me she tse le.

Sons

1st. E gra name, Me she tse le, Yonder The Sun Passes. Also Hun ka ah she, same as Hun ka u ka shon, The Hun Ka Messenger.
2nd. K shon ka name, Hun ka log ny, Good Eagle. [It would seem this name may also mean Good Earth.]
3rd. Ka shin ka name, Ah hu scah, White Wings.

Daughters

1st. Me na name, Me tsa he, Me na The Favorite.
2nd. We ha name, Me son e, White Sun.
3rd. Ah sen ka name, Hu lah me tsa he, Eagle Sacred Sun. Also Hu lah tse me, Eagle Woman.

OTHER NAMES

Male

1. Ah hu scah, White Wings.
2. Ah hu scah. Husband of E ne op pe of the Tsi shu Peace Maker clan.
3. Ah hu ko ha, Holes In The Wings. Son of Wa nah she shin ka and Moh se tsa he.
4. He lah u ka shon, Eagle That Travels. Husband of Wa tsa me of the Puma or Panther clan.
5. Hu lah pa, Eagle Head. Husband of Tsa me tsa he of the Buffalo Back clan.
6. Hu lah tun ka, Big Eagle. Husband of Pa ha pe son tsa of the Little Male Deer clan.
7. Hun ka ah she, The Hun ka Messenger.
8. Hun ka ah she. Eugene Blaine.
9. Hun ka ah she. Also Tah ha ka wa.

10. Hun ka log ny, Good Eagle.
11. Hun ka log ny. Son of Wa nah she shin ka and Hun ka me tsa he.
12. Hun ka log ny. Son of Hu lah pa and Tsa me tsa he.
13. Hun ka shin ka, Young Hun ka. [Sometimes given as Little Earth, which belongs with Maker of the Earth clan.] Son of Wa nah she shin ka and Hun ka me tsa he.
14. K she she, Never Reached Home. Husband of Ne ka of the Sun Carrier clan.
15. La bre wa hre, Slayer Of Three (war name).
16. Lookout, John. Husband of E ka moh ka of the Tsi shu Peace Maker clan.
17. Lookout, William. Son of John Lookout and E ka moh ka.
18. Me she tse le. Son of Moh se tsa he of the Tsi shu Peace Maker clan.
19. Me she tse le. Also No hu tsa le ka, No Ears. Husband of Wa kon sa moie of the Pon ka Peace Maker clan.
20. Me she tse le. Husband of Wa sha ha e of the Tsi shu Peace Maker clan.
21. Moh she ta moie, One Who Travels Above. Husband of Moh se tsa he of the Tsi shu Peace Maker clan.
22. O pah ho moie, Walking Within. Husband of Pa she he of Pa she he of the Hun ka clan.
23. Sha ka pa he, Sharp Talons. Son of Hu lah pa and Tsa me tsa he.
24. Sha ka scah, White Talons.
25. Shin ka wa sa, meaning obscure. Also Shon ka sop pe, Black Dog. Husband of Gra to me tsa he of the Men of Mystery clan.
26. Tsa he la ka, Wearer Of Buffalo Hair Head Band. (Not a gentile name.)
27. Wa ho ho, Twinkles. Son of Wa nah she shin ka and Moh se tsa he.
28. Wa ho ho. James Blaine, Jr.
29. Wa ko la, meaning obscure. Also Wa tsa he to op pe, One Whose Trophies Are Seen (war name). Son of Wa nah she shin ka and Moh se tsa he.
30. Wa kon la tun ka, Great Attacker. Husband of Me tsa he of the Elk clan.
31. Wa nah she shin ka, Little Soldier. [It would seem this would be Ah ke ta shin ka. Ah ke ta refers to the Protector of the Chief, while Wa nah she refers to the Director of the Attack.] Husband of Moh se tsa he of the Black Bear clan.
32. Wa nah she shin ka. Husband of Hun ka me tsa he of the Wind clan.
33. Wa shin pa, Bird Head. Son of Hu lah tun ka and Pa ha pe son tsa.
34. Wa shin pa. Son of Wa nah she shin ka and Hun ka me tsa he.
35. Wa sho she, Valorous. [Often given as Brave.] Husband of Moh se tsa he of the Tsi shu Peace Maker clan.
36. Wa sho she. Judge Lawrence.

Female

1. Hu lah me, Eagle Woman. Daughter of Me she tse a and Wa kon sa moie.
2. Hu lah me. Wife of Ho tsa u moie of the Night People clan.
3. Hu lah me tsa he, Eagle Sacred Sun. Daughter of Me she tse le.
4. Hu lah me tsa he. Daughter of Wa sho she and Moh se tsa tsa he.
5. Hu lah me tsa he. Wife of No pa moh le of the Buffalo Bull clan.
6. Hu lah me tsa he. Wife of Wa lum ha ke of the Tsi shu Peace Maker clan.
7. Hu lah tse me, Eagle Woman. Wife of Tsi shu shin ka of the Tsi shu Peace Maker clan.
8. Lookout, Nora. Daughter of Wa nah she shin ka and Moh se tsa he.
9. Me sa me, meaning obscure. Wife of Naranjo, a Pueblo Indian of Santa Clara, New Mexico.
10. Me son a, White Sun. Wife of Pa se to pa of the Buffalo Bull clan.
11. Me son e, White Sun.
12. Me son e. Wife of Ki he la pa she of the Men of Mystery clan.
13. Me tsa he, Sacred Sun. Daughter of Me she tse le.
14. Me tsa he. (Daughter of Shin ka wa sa.) Wife of He wa ha ka of the Puma or Panther clan.
15. Me tsa he. Daughter of Wa nah she shin ka and Hun ka me tsa he.
16. Me tsa he. Daughter of Hu lah pa and Tsa me tsa he.
17. Me tsa he. Wife of Ho ke a se of the Little Male Deer clan.
18. Me tsa he. Mother of Wa sha she me tsa he and Wa sha she of the Little Male Deer clan.
19. Me tsa he. Mother of Wa sha no pa e of the Little Male Deer clan.
20. Me tsa he. Daughter of Wa nah she shin ka and Moh se tsa he.
21. Me tsa he. Wife of Wa lo tsa ka she of the Puma or Panther clan.
22. No kon sa me, meaning obscure. Kate Whitehorn.
23. Pa she he, Reddish Head. Mary Cox.
24. Pa she he. Grace En to kah.
25. Pa she he. Prudie Martin.
26. Pa she he. Daughter of Me she tse a and Wa kon sa moie.
27. Pa she he. Wife of O pah ho moie (Ne ka sa a).
28. Pa she he. Daughter of Hu lah tun ka and Pa ha pe son tsa.
29. Pa she he. Wife of Ho mo ta ko of the Isolated Earth clan.

Clan H

HUN KA U LUM HA KA

[Last In The Hun Ka Order]

Special kinship terms and names of the first three sons and the first three daughters in a family of the Last In The Hun ka Order clan as given by Ho nah she shin ka.

Sons

1st. E gro name, Hu lah ki he ka, Eagle Chief.
2nd. K shon ka name, Tsa ka moie.
3rd. Ka Shin ka name, E pa scah, White Tail.

Daughters

1st. Me na name, Me tsa he, Me na The Favorite.
2nd. We ha name, Me son a, White Sun.
3rd. Se ka name, Me tsa he o pah, meaning obscure.

OTHER NAMES

Male

1. Ah he u ko tsa, Holes In The Wings.
2. Che to pah, Four Lodges. A valor name.
3. He pa ko ka, Blunt Horns. (This name was given to this clan as a compliment by the Buffalo Bull clan.)
4. Hu lah ne ka, Eagle Man.
5. Hu lah pa, Eagle Head.
6. Hu lah sop pe, Dark Colored Eagle.
7. Hu lah tun ka, Big Eagle.
8. Hu lah tsa he, Aged Eagle.
9. Hu lah wa sho she, Brave Eagle.
10. Hun ka, The Consecrated One. Name of the clan. [Here, La Flesche gives us a clue as to which clan he means when he refers to the Hun ka clan. He means the Last in the Hun ka Order clan.]
11. Hun ka gra she, Mottled Eagle.
12. Hun ka tun ka, Great Eagle. [Sometimes, Big Eagle. It would also seem to be Big Earth, which would refer to the Elk.]

65

13. Hun ka tse a ta, House Of The Hun ka.
14. Hu sa ta shin ka, Young Outstretched Leg. [Sometimes, Little Out-
    stretched Leg.]
15. K she she wa ha he, Causes Them To Fail To Reach Home.
16. Lum tsa ka pe, Hard To Catch.
17. Moh e she, Does Not Walk.
18. Mo se, Metal.
19. Moh she ha moie, One Who Moves Above.
20. Moh she ta moie, Moves On High.
21. Moh shon hun ka, Sacred Plume.
22. Moh ta e ha, meaning obscure.
23. Num pa se, Yellow Hands.
24. Pa hu ka shon, Hairy Head. Name given by the Buffalo Bull clan to the
    Last In The Hun ka Order clan.
25. Scah Gra, White Plumes.
26. Sha ka scah, White Talons.
27. Sha ka pa he, Sharp Talons.
28. Shin ka wa sa, meaning obscure.
29. Sho no su ka, Bends The Tree Top.
30. Shon ka sop pe, Black Dog. Lum tsa ka pe.
31. U ka se tsa, Breeze.
32. U ka shon, The Wanderer.
33. U le ka nah she, Stands Holding.
34. U le sho moie, Moves In A Circle.
35. Wa kon la tun ka, Great Attacker.
36. Wa ho ho, The Shining One.
37. Wa shin e se walla, Hated Bird. Refers to the fear of the eagle by other
    birds. [Often given as Wa she pe she or Bad Bird. A man by this name
    was called Bad Temper through misuse of the name.]
38. Wa shin pa, Bird Head.
39. Wa shin she a, Red Bird. (Red Eagle.)
40. Wa sho she, Brave.

Female

1. He ka moh ka, Feathers Blown By The Wind.
2. Hu lah me, Eagle Woman.
3. Hu lah me tsa he, Sacred Eagle Woman.
4. Hu lah tsa me, Eagle Woman.
5. Me son a, White Sun.
6. No kon sa me, meaning obscure.
7. Pa se he, Brown Head.

Clan I

O PON

[Elk]

Male

1. E a scah walla, Giver Of Speech. (A name of the Puma or Panther clan.)
2. He son ho, White Horns. Son of Moh ka sop pe and Hu lah to me.
3. Ho moh sa, meaning obscure.
4. Ho moh sa. Son of Ke moh ho and Lum ta ah sa.
5. Ho moh sa. Also Me ho shin ka. (Not ne ke a.) Husband of Moh se tsa he of the Tsi shu Peace Maker clan.
6. Ho moh sa. Son of Ho moh sa and Moh se tsa he.
7. Ke moh ho, Against The Wind. Husband of Lum ta ah sa of the Men Of Mystery clan.
8. Moh e ka shin ka, Little Clay. [Sometimes, Little Earth.] Son of Ke moh ho and Lum ta ah sa.
9. Moh ha sop pe, Black Breast. Husband of Hu lah to me of the Sun Carrier clan.
10. Moh shon ka ha, Earth Maker. Son of Ke moh ho and Lum ta ah sa.
11. O pah, Andrew. Son of Pa hu gra she of the Little Male Deer clan.

Female

1. Gro shon pa, meaning obscure. Wife of Ho ka of the Men of Mystery clan.
2. Hun ka me, Eagle Woman.
3. Hun ka me. Daughter of Moh ka sop pe and Hu lah to me.
4. Hun ka me. Daughter of Ke Moh ho and Lum ta ah sa.
5. Hun ka me. Wife of No pa walla of the Men Of Mystery clan.
6. Hun ka me. Wife of Moh sa no pa ne of the Tsi shu Peace Maker clan.
7. Lum ha wa, meaning obscure. Wife of Pe she tun ka of the Buffalo Bull clan.
8. Me tsa he, Me na The Favorite. Wife of Wa kon la tun ka.
9. Moh son ho e, meaning obscure. Daughter of Ho moh sa and Moh se tsa he.
10. Moh son ho e. Wife of Wa tsa moie of the Black Bear clan.
11. Moh sa ho e, meaning obscure. Wife of Edward Bigheart of the Pon ka Peace Maker clan.
12. Pa moh she wa gro, meaning obscure. Wife of Wa tsa ah ha of the Pon ka Peace Maker clan.

Clan J

E PA TSA

[Wind]

Male

1. Ah ka, South Wind. Son of Ka wa ho tsa and Wa to e sa a.
2. Ah ka hu a, Wind Is From The South. Son of Ka wa se and Kea sum pa.
3. E pe son ts, meaning obscure.
4. He sha ah hre, Slayer Of A Caddo. [War name.] Also Shin ka ki he ka, Young Chief. [Sometimes, Little Chief.] This name may be used by permission to honor a child. Husband of Hu lah to me of the Elder Tsi shu clan.
5. Hu lah gra she, Speckled Eagle. Son of He sha ah he and Hu lah to me.
6. Hu lah gra she. Son of Wa sop pe me of the Night People clan.
7. Hu lah ka e, Eagle Carrier. Don Dickinson.
8. Hun ka, The Sacred One. Son of Ka wah se.
9. Hun ka. Son of Hun ka.
10. Hun ka. Alfred McKinley.
11. Ka wa ho tsa, Roan Horse. (Not Ne ke a.) Also Sa sa moie, Trots As He Travels. The E pa tsa is a sub-clan of the Elk and has the right to take names relating to that animal. Husband of Wa to e sa a of the Pon ka Peace Maker clan.
12. Ka wa se, Yellow Horse. (Not Ne ke a.) Husband of Kea sum pa of the Pon ka Peace Maker clan.
13. Lum hu a, Whistle. [This is not a Ne ke a name.] Husband of Me tsa he of the Night People clan.
14. Lum hu a. Son of Ka wa ho tsa and Wa to e sa a of the Pon ka Peace Maker clan.
15. Shon ka tse a, Dog Passing By.
16. Ta tsa hu a, The Coming Wind. Son of Ka wa ho tsa and Wa to e sa a.

Female

1. Ah ka me, South Wind Woman. Daughter of He sha ah hre and Hu lah to me.
2. Ah ka me. Wife of Tah ha ka he of the Little Male Deer clan.
3. Ah ka me tsa he, South Wind Me na The Favored. Daughter of Ka wa ho tsa and Wa to e sa a.

68

4. E pa shon ka, Forked Tail Kite.
5. E pa shon ka. Wife of Ne walla of the Tsi shu Peace Maker clan.
6. E pa shon ka me, Forked Tail Kite Woman. Daughter of Hun ka.
7. E pa shon ka me. Wife of Ki he ka to of the Tsi shu Peace Maker clan.
8. E pa shon ka me. Sylvia Wood.
9. Hun ka me, Eagle Woman.
10. Hun ka me. Wife of Hu lah shu tsy of the Tsi shu Peace Maker clan.
11. Hun ka me tsa he, Hun ka Me na The Favored. Daughter of Ka wa se and Kea sum pa.
12. Hun ka me tsa he. Daughter of He sh ah hre and Hu lah to me.
13. Hun ka me tsa he. Ethel Brant.
14. Hun ka me tsa he. Wife of Wa nah she shin ka of the Hun ka clan.
15. Wa hu son e, White Bones Woman.
16. Wa hu son e. Daughter of Ka wa ho tsa and Wa to e sa a.
17. Wa hu son e. Wife of Tah he ka ha of the Little Male Deer clan.

TSI SHU GRAND DIVISION

Clan K

TSI SHU WA NUN

[Elder Tsi shu]

Male

1. E to ka wa ti an ka, Playful Wet Stone.
2. Ho sa she a, Young Street Voice. Married to a white woman.
3. Hun ka hop pe, He Who Is Called Hun ka. [Sometimes, He Who Is Called Sacred.]
4. Hun ka hop pe. Also called Wa hre, Stingy.
5. Hun ka hop pe. Son of Pa she he of the Hun ka clan.
6. Hu lah wa kon ta, Mysterious Eagle. Son of Kea sum pa of the Pon ka Peace Maker clan.
7. Hu lah wa kon ta. Son of Tsa wa hu and Son se gra.
8. Hu lah wa kon ta. Husband of Moh se tsa he of the Black Bear clan.
9. Hu lah wa kon ta. Son of O la ha moie and Moh se tsa he.
10. Hu lah wa kon ta. Son of Hu lah wa to e and He e ke op pe.
11. Hu lah wa to e, Eagle Plainly Seen.
12. Ki he ka she, Not A Chief. Son of Me tsa he hun ka wife of O ke sa.
13. Moh he sapa me tsa, Battle Axe.
14. Moie ka u ka he ne, meaning obscure. Son of O la ha moie and Moh se tsa he.
15. Ne ka e se walla, Hated Man. Husband of Ke o of the Buffalo Bull clan.
16. No hro she, Tramples The Grass. Son of E to ka wa ti an ka.
17. No pa ku a, meaning obscure. Son of O la ha moie and Moh se tsa he.
18. O la ha moie, The Follower. Husband of Moh se tsa he of the Tsi shu Peace Maker clan.
19. O sa ke a, meaning obscure.
20. Pa le wa we ta, Annoyer Of The Enemy. (War name.) Husband of Gra to me tsa he of the Men of Mystery clan.
21. Sha ka wa pe, Bloody Hands. Son of Kea sum pa of the Pon ka Peace Maker clan.
22. Shin ka wa ti an ka, Little Playful One.
23. Son tsa u gra, Dweller In Upland Forest. (Not Ne ke a.) Also We gra ka ha, Maker Of Straps. Husband of Moh shon tse e ta of the Tsi shu Peace Makere clan.
24. Tsa wa hu, Buffalo Bones. Husband of Son se gra of the Little Male Deer clan.

25. Wa e nah she, Stands Over Them.
26. Wa sha she ah ke pa, Met The Wa sha she.
27. Wa ton, meaning obscure.
28. Wa stet sy a to, Good Doctor. Son of O la ha moie and Moh se tsa he.
29. Wa tsa kon la, meaning obscure. Wa hre she says that the real name of this man is Me ka ha, Sun Maker.
30. We tse, War Club. Son of E to ka wa ti an ka.

Female

1. Dora Strike Axe. Daughter of Shin ka wa ti an ka.
2. Grace Miller. Daughter of Ho sa she a.
3. Hu lah to me, Good Eagle Woman. Wife of Wa sa to shin ka of the Tsi shu Peace Maker clan.
4. Hu lah to me. Wife of He sha ah hre or Shin ka ki he ka of the Wind clan.
5. Hu lah to me. Daughter of Pa she he of the Hun ka clan.
6. Lucy Hun ka hop pe. Daughter of Hun ka hope pe or Wa hre.
7. Me gra to me, Sun Hawk Woman.
8. Me gra to me. Daughter of Tsa wa hu and Son se gra.
9. Me gra to me. Daughter of Shin ka wa ti an ka.
10. Me gra to me. Daughter of O la ha moie and Moh se tsa he.
11. Me hun ka, Sacred Sun. Daughter of Kea sum pa of the Pon ka Peace Maker clan.
12. Me hun ka. Wife of To pa moie of the Buffalo Bull clan.
13. Moh blo pa or Moh ha pa, Corn Hill.
14. Moh blo pa. Wife of Me ka ke shin ka of the Sun Carrier clan.
15. Moh blo pa. Daughter of Hu lah wa to e and He e ke op pe.
16. Wa hre lum pa, Two Standards. [Flags.] Wife of Me ke wa ti an ka of the Sun Carrier clan.
17. Wa hre lum pa. Wife of Ne ka wa she tun ka of the Pon ka Peace Maker clan.
18. Wa hre lum pa. Wife of Tse shu ah ke pa of the Pon ka Peace Maker clan.
19. Wa hre lum pa. Wife of Pon ka wa ti an ka of the Pon ka Peace Maker clan.
20. Wa hre lum pa. Daughter of Tsa wa hu and Son se gra.
21. Wa hre lum pa. Annie Kinney.
22. Wa hre lum pa. Daughter of Hun ka hop pe and Wa hre.
23. Wa hre lum pa. Daughter of O la ha moie and Moh se tsa he.
24. Wa hre hro hro me, Standard Woman. [Flag Woman.]
25. Wa ko ki he ka, Woman Chief. (Not ne ke a.) Daughter of Shin ka wa ti an ka.
26. Wa ko sa moie, meaning obscure. Daughter of Son tsa u gra and Moh shon tse e ta.

27. Wa kon ta he lum pa, God Who Appears.
28. Wa kon ta he lum pa. Wife of Moh ha ah gra of the Isolated Earth clan.
29. Wa kon ta he lum pa. Wife of Wa le gra le ka of the Tsi shu Peace Maker clan.
30. Wa kon ta he lum pa. Wife of Me he le of the Sun Carrier clan.
31. Wa sha she me tsa he, Wa sha she Me na The Favorite. Daughter of Hu lah wa to e.
32. Wa sha she me, Wa sha she Woman. Daughter of Ne ka e se walla and Ke o.

Clan L

SEN TSA AH GRA

[Wearers Of Symbolic Locks]

Male

1. Moie ka u ka ha ne, meaning obscure. Son of U hun ka u shon and Kea sum pa.
2. Ne o pa ku a, meaning obscure. Son of U hun ka u shon and Kea sum pa.
3. U hun ka u shon, Lies At The End. Also Shon ka le he, Dog Scarer.
4. Wa hu la shu, Bone Gnawer. Son of U hun ka u shon and Kea sum pa.
5. Wa kon ta pa e, The God Who Is Feared.

Female

1. Hu lah to me, Good Eagle Woman. Daughter of U hun ka u shon and Kea sum pa.
2. Hu lah to me. Wife of Moh e ka moie of the Pon ka Peace Maker clan.
3. Wa hre lum pa, Two Standards. [Two Flags.]

Clan M

TSI SHU WA SHA TA KAH

[Tsi shu Peace Maker]

Special kinship terms and names of the first three sons and the first three daughters in a family of the Tsi shu Peace Maker clan, as given by Blo ki he ka.

Sons

1st. E gra name, Wa tse ta, meaning obscure.
2nd. K shon ka name, Ne walla, Life Giver.
3rd. Ka shin ka name, Moh sa no pa e, meaning obscure.

Daughters

1st. Me na name, Hu lah to me, Good Eagle.
2nd. We ha name, Moh se tsa he, Sacred Arrowshaft.
3rd. Ah se ka name, Moh shon tsa e ta, meaning obscure.

OTHER NAMES

Male

1. Ah hu shin ka, Little Wings. Husband of A nun to op pe of the Night People clan.
2. Ah hu shin ka. Son of O lo ha walla and Hu lah to me.
3. Blo ki he ka, Chief Of All. Husband of Wa tse u he she of the Men of Mystery clan.
4. Gra to moh se, Iron Hawk. Husband of Me tsa he of the Night People clan.
5. Gra to shin ka, Little Hawk. [Sometimes, Young Hawk.] Son of Gra to me of the Men of Mystery clan.
6. Gra moie shin ka, meaning obscure. [Gra moie has been given as Walking Hawk and Moving Hawk.] Young Claremore. Husband of Wa hre um pa of the Sun Carrier clan.
7. Ha he u me she. (Not a gentile name.) Husband of Hum pa to ka of the Pon ka Peace Maker clan.
8. Ho pa la gre, Peaceful Days. Son of Moh se no pe.
9. Ho wa sa a, meaning obscure. Husband of Ne ka ah sa of the Buffalo Bull clan.

10. Hu lah shu tsy, Red Eagle.
11. Hu lah shu tsy. Son of Pe se and Son se gra.
12. Hu lah shu tsy. Husband of Hun ka me of the Wind clan.
13. Hu lah tsa he, Aged Eagle. Son of Tsi shu hun ka and Gra to son me.
14. Hu lah tsa he. Son of Gra to me of the Men of Mystery clan.
15. Ka ha sum pa, Two Crows.
16. Ki he ka to, Standing Chief.
17. Ki he ka to. Son of Me ti an ka and To op pe.
18. Ki he ka to. Son of Pe se and Son se gra.
19. Ki he ka tun ka, Big Chief. Husband of E pa shon ka me of the Wind clan.
20. Me ti an ka, Playful Sun. Husband of Moh se tsa he of the Sun Carrier clan.
21. Me ti an ka. Husband of To op pe of the Buffalo Bull clan.
22. Moh sa no pa e, Dreaded Arrow Shaft. Son of Pa ho gra ka hre.
23. Moh se num pa, Iron Necklace.
24. Moh se num pa. Also Tsi shu wa ti an ka, Playful Tsi shu. [Sometimes, Playful is given as Saucy.] Husband of Hun ka me of the Elk clan.
25. Moh ha u gre, Sits Under A Bank. Husband of Men ko ha ka of the Men of Mystery clan.
26. Moh shon ah ke ta, Watches Over The Land. Husband of Hum pa to ka of the Pon ka Peace Maker clan.
27. Moh shon ah she a, Travels Over The Land. Son of Ki he ka to and E pa shon ka me.
28. Moh to e, The Earth.
29. Ne walla, Giver Of Life.
30. Ne walla. Son of Moh shon ah ke ta and Hum pa to ka.
31. Ne walla. Son of Gra moie shin ka and Wa gra sum pa.
32. Ne walla. Husband of E pa shon ka of the Wind clan.
33. Ne walla. Son of O la 'ha walla and Hu lah to me.
34. Num pa se, Yellow Hands. Son of Blo ki he ka.
35. Num pa se. Son of Moh shon ah ke ta and Hum pa to ka.
36. Num pa se. Son of Ha he u me she and Hum pa to ka.
37. O ke sa, meaning obscure. Husband of Me tsa he hun ka of the Isolated Earth clan.
38. O pah sho e, meaning obscure. Husband of Wa to e sa a of the Pon ka Peace Maker clan.
39. O lo ha walla, meaning obscure. Husband of Hu lah to me of the Sun Carrier clan.
40. Pa pa wa ho, Head Cutter. Son of O pa sho a and Wa to e sa a.
41. Pa pa wa ho. Son of Ne ka she a of the Little Male Deer clan.
42. Pa pa wa ho. Son of Moh sa no pa.
43. Pa pa wa ho. Son of Pe se and Son se gra.

44. Pa pa wa ho. Son of Moh shon ah ke ta and Hum pa to ka.
45. Pa pa wa ho. Son of Wa sa to shin ka. Louis Pryor.
46. Pa pa wa ho. Son of Gra to moh sa and Me tsa he.
47. Pa hu scah, White Hair. Husband of Me to op pe of the Sun Carrier clan.
48. Pe se, Acorn Of The Red Oak. Husband of Son se gra of the Pon ka Peace Maker clan.
49. Shon ka moie, Walking Dog. (War name.) This man belonged to the Bah po sub-clan of the Tsi shu Peace Maker clan. Bah po shin ka, Little Elderberry Bush, is one of the child names of this clan. Husband of Wa tsa me of the Sun Carrier clan.
50. To le ho tsa, Potato Peeler. Husband of Pa ha pe son tsa of the Little Male Deer clan.
51. To won e he, Arrives At The Village. Son of Ne walla.
52. To won e he. Husband of Tsa son me of the Buffalo Bull clan.
53. To son ka ha, Village Maker. [Also Town Maker.] Husband of Son se gra of the Little Male Deer clan.
54. Tse moie, Walks In Death. Son of Wa le gra le ka.
55. Tsi shu hun ka, Sacred Tsi shu. Husband of Gra to son me of the Men of Mystery clan.
56. Tsi shu ki he ka, Tsi shu Chief. Son of Wa sa to shin ka and Hu lah to me.
57. Tsi shu shin ka, Young Tsi shu. [Sometimes, Little Tsi shu.] Husband of Tsa me tsa he of the Buffalo Bull clan.
58. Tsi shu shin ka. Husband of Hu lah to me of the Hun ka clan.
59. Wa kon ta e a, One Who Saw Wa kon ta. Son of Wa le gra le ka.
60. Wa kon ta e a. Son of Pe se and Son se gra.
61. Wa kon ta e a. Son of Moh shon ah ke ta and Hum pa to ka.
62. Wa kon ta e a. Son of Me ti an ka and To op pe.
63. Wa kon ta e a. Son of O lo ha walla and Hu lah to me.
64. Wa le gro le ha, No Mind. (Not Ne ke a.) Also Ha pa shu tsy, Red Corn. Husband of Wa kon ta he lum pa of the Elder Tsi shu clan.
65. Wa lo ha ka, Clutches Them Till They Cry. Husband of Hu lah me tsa he of the Hun ka clan.
66. Wa ne a to, Giver Of Life. Son of Me ti an ka and Moh se tsa he.
67. Wa ne a to. Son of Gra to me of the Men of Mystery clan.
68. Wa ne a to. Son of Ha he u me she and Hum pa to ka.
69. Wa ne a to. Husband of Wa kon sa moie of the Pon ka Peace Maker clan.
70. Wa sa to shin ka, meaning obscure. Husband of Hu lah to me of the Elder Tsi shu clan.
71. Wa sa to shin ka. Louis Pryor.
72. Wa shin ka sop pe, Black Bird. Husband of To op pe of the Buffalo Bull clan.
73. Wa shin ka he, Bird Feathers. Son of Shon ka moie.

74. Wa stet sy a to, Good Doctor. Son of Pa ho gra ka hre and Hu lah to me.
75. Wa stet sy a to. Son of Ah hu she a and E no to op pe.
76. Wa stet sy a to. Son of Blo ki he ka.
77. Wa stet sy a to. Husband of Wa hre lo pa of the Elder Tsi shu clan.
78. Wa stet sy a to. Son of Tsi shu hun ka.
79. Wa stet sy a to. Son of Moh shon ah ke ta and Hum pa to ka.
80. Wa stet sy a to. Son of Num pa se and Wa sha she me tsa he.
81. Wa stet sy a to. Son of Ha he u me she and Hum pa to ka.
82. Wa stet sy a to. Son of To le hro tsa and Pa ha pe son tsa. [See 84 below.]
83. Wa stet sy a to. Son of Moh sa no pa and Hun ka me.
84. Wa stet sy a to. Son of To le hro tsa and Pa ha pe son tsa. [Possibly a repeat of 82 or another son.]
85. Wa stet sy a to. Son of Moh sa no pe and Hun ka me.

Female

1. A non to op pe, One Seen By All. Daughter of Tsi shu hun ka and Gra to son me.
2. A non to op pe. Daughter of No pa se and Wa sha she me tsa he.
3. A non to op pe. Daughter of Gra to moh sa and Me tsa he.
4. A non to op pe. Daughter of O lo ka walla and Hu lah to me.
5. Daisy Ware. Daughter of Ha he u me she and Hum pa to ka.
6. E ka moh ka, same as He ka moh ka. [Eagle Down.] Daughter of Pa hu scah and Me to op pe.
7. E ka moh ka. Wife of John Lookout of the Hun ka clan.
8. E ne op pe, Protector. Daughter of Pa hun ka ka gre and Hu lah to me.
9. E ne op pe. Annie Daniels.
10. E ne op pe. Daughter of Blo ki he ka.
11. E ne op pe. Daughter of Me ti an ka and To op pe.
12. E ne op pe. Wife of Ah hu scah of the Hun ka clan.
13. E ne op pe. Daughter of Hu lah shu tsy and Hun ka me.
14. Gra to me, Hawk Woman. Daughter of Pa hu scah and Me to op pe.
15. Gra to me. Daughter of Ne ka shu a of the Little Male Deer clan.
16. He ah ke op pe, Eagle Down. Wife of Gra k she of the Sun Carrier clan.
17. He ah ke op pe. Daughter of Me ti an ka and Moh se tsa he.
18. He ah ke op pe. Granddaughter of Wa kon ta he o pa, wife of Moh ha ah gra.
19. He ah ke op pe. Daughter of Tsi shu hun ka and Gra to son me.
20. He ah ke op pe. Wife of Tsa to ah tun ka of the Buffalo Bull clan.
21. He ah ke op pe. Daughter of Me ti an ka and To op pe.
22. He a ke op pe. Wife of Wa kon ta tse a of the Little Male Deer clan.
23. He ah ke op pe. Wife of Hu lah wa to e of the Elder Tsi shu clan.

24. He ka moh ka, Eagle Down.
25. He ka moh ka. Daughter of Me ti an ka and To op pe.
26. He ka moh ka. Daughter of O lo ha walla and Hu lah to me.
27. Hu lah to me, Good Eagle Woman. Daughter of Pa hu scah and Me to op pe.
28. Hu lah to me. Wife of Son tsa ko ha of the Little Male Deer clan.
29. Hu lah to me. Wife of Wa hre she of the Puma or Panther clan.
30. Hu lah to me. Wife of No ka to ho of the Men of Mystery clan. (Daughter of Shon ka moie.)
31. Hu lah to me. Wife of Pon ka shin ka of the Pon ka Peace Maker clan.
32. Hu lah to me. Daughter of Ho wa sa a and Ne ka ah sa.
33. Hu lah to me. Daughter of To won ka he and Son se gra.
34. Hu lah to me. Daughter of No ko sa me of the Hun ka clan.
35. Hu lah to me. Daughter of Ne walla.
36. Hu lah to me. Augustine Crow.
37. Hu lah to me. Wife of Ne ka wa ti an ka of the Sun Carrier clan.
38. Hu lah to me. Daughter of Moh shon ah ke ta and Hum pa to ka.
39. Hu lah to me. Daughter of Me ti an ka and To op pe.
40. Hu lah to me. Daughter of Ha he u me she and Hum pa to ka.
41. Hu lah to me. Daughter of Wa ne a to and Wa kon sa moie.
42. Hu lah to me. Daughter of Ne walla and E pa shon ka.
43. Hu lah to me. Wife of Ko she se gra of the Pon ka Peace Maker clan.
44. Hu lah to me. Wife of Lo tsa tun ka of the Pon ka Peace Maker clan.
45. Hu lah to me. Daughter of To le hro tsa and Pa ha pe son tsa.
46. Hu lah to me. Wife of Ka he ka nah she of the Little Male Deer clan.
47. Hu lah to me. Wife of Ah ke ta shin ka of the Little Male Deer clan.
48. Mary Cox. Daughter of Ah hu she a and A non to Op pe.
49. Moh se tsa he, Sacred Arrow Shaft. Wife of Moh she ta moie. (This is a Puma or Panther clan name.)
50. Moh se tsa he. Wife of Wa sho she of the Hun ka clan.
51. Moh se tsa he. Wife of Ke le ko pe of the Pon ka Peace Maker clan.
52. Moh se tsa he. Daughter of Moh sa no pa.
53. Moh se tsa he. Wife of Ho mo sa of the Elk clan.
54. Moh se tsa he. Wife of O la ha moie of the Elder Tsi shu clan.
55. Moh se tsa he. Daughter of O ke sa and Me tsa he hun ka.
56. Moh shon tse e ta, Born On The Earth. Daughter of Pe se and Son se gra.
57. Moh shon tse e ta. Daughter of Wa sa to shin ka and Hu lah to me.
58. Moh shon tse e ta. Wife of Wa she wa ha of the Pon ka Peace Maker clan.
59. Moh shon tse e ta. Wife of Son tsa u gre or We e ka ha.
60. Pa hu le shon, meaning obscure. Daughter of Moh shon ah ke ta.
61. Wa ko ki he ka, Woman Chief. (Not a gentile name.)
62. Wa ko ki he ka. Wife of Hu lah hre of the Pon ka Peace Maker clan.

63. Wa sa op pe, meaning obscure. Daughter of Moh sa no pa.
64. Wa sha he e, meaning obscure. Wife of Tsa to ka en tsa of the Buffalo Bull Face clan.
65. Wa sha he e. [Customarily the final "e" was omitted. This was especially true if the preceding syllable ended in "e".] Wife of Me she tse le of the Hun ka clan.
66. Wa sop pe me, Black Bear Woman. Daughter of No pa se and Wa sha she me tsa he.

Clan N

TSA TO KA EN TSA

[Buffalo Bull Face]

Male

1. Hun ka hop pe, Taken For A Hun ka.
2. Hun ka hop pe. Son of Tsa to ka en tsa and Wa sha ha e.
3. Hu lah wa kon ta, Mysterious Eagle. Son of Hum pa to ka of the Pon ka Peace Maker clan.
4. Tsa pa u le ka, Holder Of The Buffalo Head.
5. Tsa to ka en tsa, Buffalo Bull Face. Husband of Wa sha ha e of the Tsi shu Peace Maker clan.
6. Wa ke ah ha ka, Tied Together.
7. Wa sha ah ke pa, Met The Wa sha she. Son of Wa to ka and E ne op pe.
8. Wa to ka, Active. Husband of E ne op pe of the Tsi shu Peace Maker clan.

Female

1. Hu lah to me, Good Eagle Woman. Daughter of Hum pa to ka of the Pon ka Peace Maker clan.
2. Hu lah to me. Daughter of Tsa to ka en tsa and Wa sha he e.
3. Kea sum me, meaning obscure. Daughter of Hum pa to ka of the Pon ka Peace Maker clan.

Clan O

TSA TUN KA

[Big Buffalo]

(Only one of this clan survives.)

Tsa me tsa he, Sacred Buffalo Woman. Wife of Hu lah pe of the Hun ka clan.
[La Flesche indicates this was the last surviving member of this clan.]

Clan P

ME KE

[Sun Carrier]

Special kinship terms and personal names of the first three sons and the first three daughters in a family of the Sun Carrier clan, as given by A hu gra, a member of the clan.

Sons

1st. E gra name, Hun ka hop pe, Mistaken For A Hun ka.
2nd. K shon name, Gra to ka ha, Hawk Maker.
3rd. Ka shin ka name, Me he la, Sun Down; also, Me he le shin ka, Little Sun Down.

Daughters

1st. Me na name, Hu lah to me, Good Eagle Woman.
2nd. We ha name, Me to op pe, Sun That Is Looked At.
3rd. Se ka or Ah sen ka name, Me ke me, Sun Carrier Woman.

OTHER NAMES

Male

1. E ke hop pa she, Lost. Son of E to moie and Wa to e sa a.
2. E to moie, meaning obscure. Husband of Wa to e sa a of the Pon ka Peace Maker clan.
3. George. Son of Me he la and Wa kon ta to pa.
4. Gra to ah ha, Hawk Maker.
5. Gra to wa kon, Mystery Hawk. Son of E to moie and Wa to e sa a.
6. Gre k she, The Returned. Husband of He e ke op pe of the Tsi shu Peace Maker clan.
7. Ho e ka she, meaning obscure. Son of Me ka ka shin ka and Moh blo pa.
8. Hun ka hop pe, Mistaken For A Hun ka.
9. Hun ka hop pe. Son of Me ka ka shin ka and Moh blo pa.
10. Hun ka hop pe. Son of Me he la and Wa kon ta he to pa.
11. Hun ka hop pe. Son of Me lo to moie shin ka and Pa hu a sa.
12. John. Son of Me he la and Wa kon ta he to pa.

13. Me he la, Sunset. [Sometimes, Sun Down.] Husband of Wa kon ta he to pa of the Elder Tsi shu clan.
14. Me ka ka shin ka, Little Star. Husband of Moh blo pa of the Elder Tsi shu clan.
15. Me ke wa ti an ka, Playful Sun Carrier. Husband of Wa hra to pa of the Elder Tsi shu clan.
16. Me ke wa ti an ka. Also A hu gra, Elm Creek. Also Pa ka ha she, Never Beaten. Husband of Hu lah to me of the Tsi shu Peace Maker clan.
17. Me lo to moie shin ka, Young Mid Day. Husband of Pa hu a sa.
18. Shon e ne la, Clings To Tree For Safety. Also Ka ha ah gro, Crow Head Dress.
19. To e ka she, Moon Returned To Sight. Son of Me ke wa ti an ka and Wa hra to pa.
20. Wa sha ah ke pa, Met The Wa sha she. Son of Me lo to moie and Wa to e sa a.
21. Wa shin ka log ny, Good Bird.
22. Wa shon ke la, Met Them By Chance. (Hall Good.)

Female

1. Hu lah to me, Good eagle Woman. Wife of Moh ka sop pe of the Elk clan.
2. Hu lah to me. Wife of E sta moh sa of the Puma or Panther clan.
3. Hu lah to me. Wife of O lo ha la of the Tsi shu Peace Maker clan.
4. Me ka shon e, Sun That Travels. Daughter of Me lo to moie and Wa to e sa a.
5. Moh se tsa he, Sacred Arrow Shaft.
6. Moh se tsa he. Wife of Mew ti an ka of the Tsi shu Peace Maker clan.
7. Me to op pe, Sun Looked Upon. Wife of Pa hu scah of the Tsi shu Peace Maker clan.
8. Me to op pe. Daughter of Me ke wa ti an ka and Wa hra to pa.
9. Ne ka, Person. [Also Man.] Wife of Ka she she of the Hun ka clan.
10. To op pe, Looked Upon. Daughter of E to moie and Wa to e sa a.
11. Wa hra to pa, Two Standards. [Sometimes, Two Flags.]
12. Wa tsa me, Star Woman. Wife of Shon ka moie of the Tsi Peace Maker clan.

Clan Q

HUN E NE KA SHE KA

[Night People]

Special kinship terms and personal names of the first three sons and the first three daughters in a family of the Night People clan, as given by Ne ka to pa, a member of the clan.

Sons

1st. E gro name, Ho moie, Moves In The Night.
2nd. K shon ka name, Tse shu u thu ha ka, Last In The Order Of The Tsi shu.
3rd. Ka shin ka name, Hun ka e ta she, Not Of The Hun ka. Also Hum pa hu, Day Comes.

Daughters

1st. Me na name, Me tsa he, Me na The Favorite.
2nd. We ha name, Ho wa ko, Night Woman.
3rd. Se ka or Ah sen ka name, A non to op pe, Only One That Is Seen By All.

OTHER NAMES

Male

1. Ho moie, Travelling Night. Son of Ne ka to pa.
2. Ho moie. Andrew Jackson.
3. Ho tsa u moie, Walks Among Cedars. Husband of Hu lah me of the Hun ka clan.
4. Hum pa hu, Day Comes. Husband of Hum pa to ka of the Little Male Deer clan.
5. Hum pa hu. Husband of Son se gra of the Pon ka Peace Maker clan.
6. Hun ka ah ka she, meaning obscure. Son of Wa sha she me tsa he, wife of No pa se.
7. Hun ka ah ka she. Son of To ta ah sa of the Men of Mystery clan.
8. Ne ka ah ke pa no, Runs To Meet Men. Also A she ka hre, Slew The Wrong Man. (War name.) Husband of Gra to me tsa he of the Men of Mystery clan.
9. Ne ka to pa, Two Men.

10. Pa tsa moie, Fire Walker. Husband of We tse to sa of the Isolated Earth clan.
11. Sho tsa, Smoke. Son of Ne ka ah ke pa no and Gra to me tsa he.
12. Sin tsa le ka, No Tail. Hayes Little Bear. [Hayes Little Bear's daughter, Sophia Little Bear Dahlberg, gives her father's name as Ha ma ge and her brother, Harold Little Bear's name as Sin tsa le ka.]
13. We sop pe she, meaning obscure. Son of Ne ka ah ke pa no and Gra to me tsa he.

Female

1. A non op pe, Only One Seen By All. Wife of Ah hu she a of the Tsi shu Peace Maker clan.
2. Ho to wa ko, Woman Of The Night.
3. Me to pa, Sees The Sun. Daughter of Ne ka ah ke pa no and Me tsa he, Me na The Favorite. Wife of La su a of the Wind clan.
4. Me tsa he, Me na The Favorite. Wife of Gra to moh sa of the Tsi shu Peace Maker clan.
5. Me tsa he. Daughter of To ta ah sa of the Men of Mystery clan.
6. Me tsa he. Wife of Le he pe of the Little Male Deer clan.
7. Ne ka she tse la, meaning obscure. Wife of Che she walla of the Little Male Deer clan.
8. Wa sop pe me, Black Bear Woman. Lucy H. Bangs.

The following are special kinship terms and personal names of the first three sons and the first three daughters in a family of this clan, Night People, as given by Ho moie a member of the clan.

Sons

1st. E gro name, Ho moie, Traveling Night.
2nd. K shon ka name, Sho tsa, Smoke.
3rd. Ka shin ka name, Ta ko e ka, No Sinews.

Daughters

1st. Me na name, Me na The Favorite.
2nd. ------ name, Wa sop pe me, Black Bear Woman.
3rd. Se ka name, A non to op pe, Seen By All.

Male

14. Ho gre, Night Has Returned.
15. Ho ka he a go, Hair Like Badger's.
16. Hun ka le ka she, meaning obscure.
17. Mo ko, Medicine.
18. O ko tse wa sha ko, Struggles By Himself.
19. O pah stet sy, Long Body.
20. Pa se, Brown Nose.
21. Se la tsa ho tsa, Gray Heels.
22. Sha bla scah, Flat Hands.
23. Ta ko moie, Walks As In Fire.
24. To to gre nah she, Stands Upright.
25. Wa ha ha ta, Shaggy Hair.
26. Wa she sha to ka, Soft Fat.
27. Wa sop a wa kon ta ke, Mysterious Bear.
28. Wa sop a shin ka, Little Bear.

Female

9. Ho wa ko, Night Woman.
10. Me shon ka, meaning obscure.
11. Ne ka she tsa le, Persons Passes By.
12. Wa hra to pa, Two Standards. [Flags.]

Clan R

NE KA WA KON TA KE

[Men Of Mystery]

Special kinship terms and personal names of the first three sons and the first three daughters of a family of the Men of Mystery clan. The Thunder is the life symbol of this clan.

Sons

1st. E gro name, Gra to tsa ka, New Hawk. Also Gra to ho a, Gray Hawk.
2nd. K shon ka name, Gra to scah, White Hawk.
3rd. Ka shin ka name, Ne u tse gra, Rumbling In The Distance. Also Ho ta moie, Roars As He Comes.

Daughters

1st. Me na name, Gra to me tsa ha, New Hawk Woman.
2nd. We ha name, To ta ah sa, meaning obscure.
3rd. Se ka name, Gra to me shin ka, Little Hawk Woman.

OTHER NAMES

Male

1. Ah gre ha la, Returns To His Place.
2. Ah ke ta ki he ka, Chief Protector.
3. Gra to scah, White Hawk. (K shon ka name.) Son of No ka to ho and Hu lah to me of the Tsi shu Peace Maker clan.
4. Gra to scah. Husband of Me ka sho e of the Pon ka Peace Maker clan.
5. Gra to scah. Son of Gra to scah and Me ka sho e.
6. Gra to scah. Son of We to ha en ka and Hum pa to ka.
7. Gra to scah. Son of No pa wala and Hun ka me.
8. Gra to tsa ka, New Hawk. (E gro name.)
9. Gra tse a, Hawk Passing By. Son of To won ka she and Hu lah to me.
10. Gre nah she, Returns And Stands.
11. Ho ka, Initiator. (Not a gentile name.) Husband of Gro shon pa of the Elk clan.
12. Ho tsa u moie, Dwell Among The Cedars.
13. Hu a ke ta, Comes Roaring.

14. Hu a no she, Stands Soughing.
15. Ka la moie, Clear Day Approaching.
16. Ka no ho ha, Cracks The Turtle With His Foot.
17. Ke he la pa she, Self Confident.
18. Me ka shin ka, Little Raccoon. [Also Young Coon.]
19. Me ka wa ti an ka, Playful Raccoon. [Also Saucy Coon.]
20. Me tso shin ka, Little Grizzly Bear.
21. Moh ha pe moie, Travelling Cloud.
22. Moh ka se, Yellow Breast.
23. Ne shu moie, Travelling Rain.
24. Ne shu tun ka, Big Rain.
25. No ka to ho, Blue Back. Also Me ka shin ka. [Little Coon.] Husband of Hu lah to me of the Tsi shu Peace Maker clan.
26. No pa walla, Fear Inspiring. [Sometimes, Thunder Fear or Causes Them To Be Afraid.] Husband of Hun ka me of the Elk clan.
27. O pa le a, meaning obscure. Saucy Calf thinks it is a valor name.
28. Pa ne wa ha pa le, Poor Pawnee.
29. Pa su tun ka, Big Hail.
30. Prat, Charles. Son of No pa walla and Hun ka me.
31. Sa sa ke ta, Returns Trotting.
32. Sha wa pe, Bloody Hands.
33. She lo tsa we tse, Strikes With The Knee.
34. Shon ka hre, Tree Killer.
35. Shon u le stet sy ka, Tree Splitter.
36. To won ka she, Taker Of Towns. Husband of Hu lah to me of the Elder Tsi shu clan.
37. Wa ho pa shin ka, Little Shrine.
38. Wa hu ka hre, Strikes The Bones. Valor name.
39. Wa lo ta sa, Crashing Sound.
40. Wa shin ne ka, Bird Man.
41. We to ha en ka, meaning obscure. Husband of Hum pa to ka of the Little Male Deer clan.

Female

1. E shon pa, meaning obscure. Daughter of Moh se tsa he of the Puma or Panther clan.
2. Gra to son me, White Hawk Woman. Wife of Tsi shu hun ka of the Tsi shu Peace Maker clan.
3. Gra to me tsa he, Hawk Me na The Favorite.
4. Gra to me tsa he. Wife of Shin ka wa sa of the Hun ka clan.
5. Gra to me tsa he. Wife of Pe she tun ka of the Buffalo Bull clan.

6. Gra to me tsa he. Daughter of No pa walla and Hun ka me.
7. Gra to me, Hawk Woman.
8. Gra to me tsa he, Hawk Me na The Favorite. Daughter of We to ha en ka and Hum pa to ka.
9. Ho ta me, Black Bird Woman. Daughter of Wa ko sa moie of the Pon ka Peace Maker clan.
10. Ho tsa me, Cedar Woman.
11. Me tsu ha ka, meaning obscure. Wife of Moh ha u gre of Tsi shu Peace Maker clan.
12. To ta ah sa, meaning obscure. Daughter of Wa kon sa moie of the Pon ka Peace Maker clan.
13. To ta ah sa. Daughter of Ke he la pa she and Me son e.
14. To ta ah sa. Wife of Ke moh ho of the Elk clan.
15. Wa tse u he she, meaning obscure. Wife of Blo ki he ka of the Tsi shu Peace Maker clan.

Clan S

LO HA

[Buffalo Bull]

Special kinship terms and personal names of the first three sons and the first three daughters in a family of the Buffalo Bull clan, as given by Saucy Calf.

Sons

1st. E gro name, Kon sa wa a, meaning obscure.
2nd. K shon ka name, He pa sa ta, Sheds His Hair.
3rd. Ka shin ka name, Tsa she hun ka, Sacred Calf.

Daughters

1st. Me na name, To op pe, Gazed Upon. Also Lo ha me, Buffalo Bull Woman.
2nd. We ha name, Pa hu le shon, Shaggy Head.
3rd. Se ka or Ah sen ka name, Tsa me se, Brown Buffalo Woman. [Sometimes, Reddish Buffalo Woman.] Also Po ke ta, the Lowing Herd. Also Tsa me hre, Real Buffalo Woman.

OTHER NAMES

Male

1. Ah he us ha she he, Red Forelegs.
2. Ah ka ha moie, Walks Outside.
3. Ah ka shon, Bushy.
4. E he u pa to, Pointed Beard.
5. E la no sa, Head Them Off.
6. E sha ka ta pe, Playful. Refers to the sport of hunting buffalo.
7. E wa sha ko, Dependable. Valor name. Also Shon ka u ke pa tsa, Wolf Robe. [Also a valor name.]
8. Fletcher, Francis. Son of Lo ha shin ka and Me son a.
9. Gre to stet sy tsa, Long Hawk. Son of Lo ha shin ka and Kea sum pa.
10. Ha pa to ha, Stubby Horns.
11. He se moie, Brown Hair Walker. Also Se ha, Soles.
12. Hu gra tun ka, Big Legs.
13. Ka tse gre lo, Crosses.

14. Ke no to, Springs Forth. Valor name. Also Tsa moh ke u a, meaning obscure. Son of Me hun ka of the Elder Tsi shu clan.
15. La sa ha ka, Rough Tongue.
16. Le ha pa she, Not Chased.
17. Le ha pe ah ke she, Thinks Himself Chased.
18. Lo ha ki he ka, Buffalo Bull Chief.
19. Lo ha shin ka, Young Buffalo Bull. [Sometimes, Little Buffalo Bull.] Also Wa to e ke le, Comes To View. (A Sun Carrier name.) Husband of Me son a of the Black Bear clan.
20. Lo ha shin ka. Husband of Kea sum pa of the Pon ka Peace Maker clan.
21. Lo ha wa kon ta, The Mystic Buffalo Bull.
22. Lo ha wa ti an ka, Mischievous Buffalo Bull. [Sometimes, Playful Buffalo Bull or Saucy Buffalo Bull.]
23. Louis. Son of Pa se to pa and Me son a.
24. Men tsa ko, Bow String. Son of Tsa to ah tun ka and He e ke op pe.
25. Moh e gra to, Walks Home. Son of Tsa to ah tun ka and He e ke op pe.
26. Moh ka shu tsy or Moh ka shu a, Dust Makers. [Sometimes, Red Dust Makers.] Also Pe she u la ha, Grass Clings To Him. Husband of Wa to e sa a of the Little Male Deer clan.
27. Moh shon u ka shon. Wanderer. [Sometimes, Wanders Over The Land.]
28. Ne ka hu a, Roaring Waters.
29. No ka ah pa sha ta, Straddles The Back.
30. No pa moh le, Two Walking. Husband of Hu lah me tsa he of the Hun ka clan.
31. No pa walla, Fear Inspiring. [Sometimes, Thunder Fear or Causes Them To Be Afraid.] This name is used by both this and the Men Of Mystery clan.
32. No she tse a, Rises Suddenly.
33. O pah so shin ka, Small Hips.
34. Pa se to pa, Four Hills. Husband of Wa sha she me tsa he of the Little Male Deer clan.
35. Pa se to pa. Husband of Me son a of the Hun ka clan.
36. Pa she ah tsa, Grass Eater.
37. Pa ta he sha ke a, Hairy Head.
38. Pe she gre nah she, Returns To Fight.
39. Pe she tun ka, Big Bad One. Husband of Gra to me tsa he of the Men of Mystery clan.
40. Pe she tun ka. Husband of Mary of the Elk clan.
41. Se ha, Soles.
42. Se ha. Son of Lo he shin ka and Kea sum pa.
43. Sen tsa shin ka, Little Tail.
44. Sen tsa so ta, Slender Tail.

45. Sen tsa wa kon ta, Mystic Tail.
46. Sen tsa wa kon ta. Son of Tsa sa tun ka and Wa kon sa moie.
47. Sen tsa wa kon ta. Son of No pa moh le and Hu lah me tsa he.
48. Sen tsa wa kon ta. Son of Me ka sho e, wife of Moh she scah ke ka hre.
49. Se tun ka, Big Feet. [Sometimes, Big Foot.]
50. Sha pa nah she, Stands Dark.
51. To pa moh le, Walk By Fours. Husband of Me Hun ka of the Elder Tsi shu clan.
52. To pa moh le. Son of Lo ha shin ka and Kea sum pa.
53. To pa tse, Swollen.
54. Tsa le tse, Buffalo Ribs.
55. Tsa moh ke le, meaning obscure.
56. Tsa pa shin ka, Little Buffalo Head. Husband of Wa sop pe wa ko of the Black Bear clan.
57. Tsa sa tun ka, Big Belly. Husband of Wa kon sa moie of the Pon ka Peace Maker clan.
58. Tsa sen tsa, Buffalo Tail.
59. Tsa shin ka wa ti an ka, Playful Calf. [Usually given as Saucy Calf.] Also Ha ka walla, Makes Them Weep.
60. Tsa to ah moie, Walking Bull. [Also Tsa to ka moie.]
61. Tsa to ah tun ka, Big Bull. [Also Tsa to ka tun ka.]
62. Tsa to ah shin ka, Little Bull.
63. Tsa to ka, Buffalo Bull.
64. U ka ha ha pa, Bushy Head.
65. U ke pa to, Rolls Himself.
66. U ko tse nah she, Stands Alone.
67. U la ka pe, Famed. Valor name.
68. U me she, Bedding.
69. Wa no ka, Stampede.
70. We she u ke pe, Trench Full.
71. Wa stet sy ha, Strip Of Meat.
72. Wa u we se, Jumper.

Female

1. E to moie, meaning uncertain. A Sun Carrier clan name. Daughter of Lo ha shin ka and Me se a of the Black Bear clan.
2. E to won gro pe, One For Whom Villages Are Built. Daughter of Tsa pa shin ka and Wa sop pe wa ko of the Black Bear clan.
3. Ke o, Wounded. Wife of Ne ka e se walla of the Elder Tsi shu clan.
4. Lo ha me, Buffalo Bull Woman.
5. Ne ka ah sa, meaning uncertain.

6. Ne ka ah sa. Wife of Ho wa sa a of the Tsi shu Peace Maker clan.
7. Ne ka ah sa. Daughter of Tsa sa tun ka and Wa ko moie of the Pon ka Peace Maker clan.
8. Pa hu le shon, Shaggy Head.
9. Pa hu le shon. Daughter of Pa se to pa and Me son a of the Hun ka clan.
10. Po ku ta, Lowing.
11. Po ku ta. Daughter of Tsa to ah tun ka and He e ke op pe of the Tsi shu Peace Maker clan.
12. Po ku ta. Wife of Kon sa hun ka of the Isolated Earth clan.
13. To op pe, Gazed Upon. [Also Looked Upon.]
14. To op pe. Wife of Me ti an ka of the Tsi shu Peace Maker clan.
15. To op pe. Wife of Wa shin ka sop pe of the Tsi shu Peace Maker clan.
16. Tsa e kon la, meaning uncertain.
17. Tsa hun ka me, Sacred Buffalo Woman. Daughter of Tsa to ah tun ka and He e ke op pe of the Tsi shu Peace Maker clan.
18. Tsa me hre, Red Buffalo Woman. Wife of Tsi shu shin ka of the Tsi shu Peace Maker clan.
19. Tsa me hun ka, Buffalo Sacred Cow. Wife of Hun ka la gre of the Hun ka clan.
20. Tsa me se, Brown Buffalo Woman.
21. Tsa me se. Daughter of He se moie.
22. Tsa me se. Daughter of Lo ha shin ka and Kea sum pa of the Pon ka Peace Maker clan.
23. Tsa son me, White Buffalo Woman. Wife of To won e he of the Tsi shu Peace Maker clan.
24. Tsa son me. Daughter of Lo ha shin ka and Kea sum pa of the Pon ka Peace Maker clan.

INDEX FOR OSAGE NAMES BY CLAN

[Indexed in Osage – American Phonics]

USER NOTE: Each listed clan is headed by an alphabetical letter such as Clan A, Clan B, etc., through S. All index numbers start with a capital letter which refers to the clan letter. The list is numbered sequentially under Male and under Female headings. To direct the user to a male or female number, a small "m" or small "f" is used after the capital letter. This is followed by an arabic number which refers to the numbered names in the male or female list. Thus, Hm12 would direct the user to Clan H or Hun ka u lum ha ka clan, and the male list, number 12, which is hun ka tun ka. Likewise, Kf26 would refer the user to Clan K or Tsi shu wa num clan, female list, number 26 or Wa ko sa moie.

A

A nom me tsa to	Bm2,Bm3, Bm4,Cm1
A non op pe	Qf1
A non to op pe	Mf1,Mf2, Mf3,Mf4
A she ka hre	Qm8
Ah gre ha la	Rm1
Ah he u ko tsa	Hm1
Ah he us ha she he	Sm1
Ah hu ko ha	Gm3
Ah hu scah	Gm1,Gm2
Ah hu shin ka	Mm1,Mm2
Ah hu to pa	Df1
Ah ka	Jm1
Ah ka ha moie	Sm2
Ah ka hu a	Jm2
Ah ka me	Jf1,Jf2
Ah ka me tsa he	Jf3
Ah ka shon	Sm3
Ah ke ta ki he ka	Rm2
Ah ke ta shin ka	Bm1,Gm31
Ah pa shin ka	Am12

(A ends here)

B

Bangs, Lucy H.	Qf8
Blo ki he ka	Mm3

C

Che she walla	Bm5,Cm2
Che to pah	Hm2
Cox, Mary	Mf48

E

E a scah walla	Im1
E gra ka shin ka	Em1
E he u pa to	Sm4
E ho la pa e	Dm1
E ka moh ka	Mf6,Mf7
E ke hop pa she	Pm1
E la no sa	Sm5
E ne op pe	Mf8,Mf9,Mf10, Mf11,Mf12,Mf13
E pa shon ka	Jf4,Jf5
E pa shon ka me	Jf6,Jf7,Jf8
E pa shu tsy	Em2
E pe son ts	Jm3

E (cont.)

E sha ka ta pe Sm6
E shon pa Rf1
E stah mo sa Em3
E stah pa tsa Cm3
E stah sop pe Fm1
E to ka wa ti an ka Km1
E to moie Pm2,Sf1
E to won gro pe Sf2
E wa sha ko Sm7

F

Fletcher, Francis Sm9

G

George Pm3
Good, Hall Pm22
Gra e gro le ke Am1
Gra moie shin ka Mm6
Gra to ah ha Pm4
Gra to me Mf14,Mf15,Rf7
Gra to me shin ka Bf1
Gra to me tsa he Rf3,Rf4, Rf5,Rf6,Rf8
Gra to moh se Mm4
Gra to scah Rm3,Rm4,Rm5, Rm6,Rm7
Gra to shin ka Mm5
Gra to son me Rf2
Gra to tsa ka Rm8
Gra to wa kon Pm5
Gra to wa kon la Am2
Gra tse a Rm9
Gre k she Pm6
Gre nah she Rm10
Gro shon pa If1

(G ends here)

H

Ha he u me she Mm7
Ha ka walla Sm59
Ha pa shu tsy Mm64
Ha pa to ha Sm10
He ah ke op pe Mf16,Mf17, Mf18,Mf19,Mf20, Mf21,Mf22,Mf23
He ka moh ka Hf1,Mf6,Mf24, Mf25,Mf26
He la u ka shon Gm4
He lo ka le Am3,Am4
He pa ko ka Hm3
He scah moie Cm4
He se moie Sm11
He sha ah hre Jm4
He son ho Im2
He wa ha ka Fm2
Ho bla scah shin ka Cm5
Ho e ka she Pm7
Ho Gre Qm14
Ho he ha Cm6
Ho ho Bm6
Ho ho a Bm7
Ho ka Rm11
Ho ka ha Cm7
Ho ka he a go Qm15
Ho ke a se Cm8
Ho ke ah se Bm8,Bm9,Bm10
Ho moh sa Im3,Im4,Im5,Im6
Ho moie Qm1,Qm2
Ho pa Cm9
Ho pa la gre Mm9
Ho sa she a Km2
Ho scah Cm10
Ho son Bm11,Cm11
Ho ta me Rf9
Ho to wa ko Qf2
Ho tsa me Rf10
Ho tsa u moie Qm3,Rm12
Ho wa he Cm12

Ho wa ko	Qf9
Ho wa sa a	Mm9
Hu a ke ta	Rm13
Hu a no she	Rm14
Hu gra tun ka	Sm12
Hu la pa	Hm5
Hu lah gra she	Jm5,Jm6
Hu lah ka e	Jm7
Hu lah me	Gf1,Gf2
Hu lah me tsa he	Gf3,Gf4,
	Gf5,Gf6,Hf3
Hu lah ne ka	Hm4
Hu lah pa	Gm5
Hu lah shu tsy	Mm10,Mm11,
	Mm12
Hu lah sop pe	Hm6
Hu lah to me	Af1,Kf3,Kf4,
	Kf5,Lf1,Lf2,Mf27,Mf28,
	Mf29,Mf30,Mf31,Mf32,Mf33,
	Mf34,Mf35,Mf36,Mf37,Mf38,
	Mf39,Mf40,Mf41,Mf42,Mf43,
	Mf44;Mf45,Mf46,Mf47,Nf1,
	Nf2,Pf1,Pf2,Pf3
Hu lah tsa me	Gf7,Hf4,Hm8,
	Mm13,Mm14
Hu lah tse	Am5
Hu lah tun ka	Gm6,Hm7
Hu lah wa kon ta	Km6,Km7,
	Km8,Km9,Km10,Nm3
Hu lah wa sho she	Hm9
Hu lah wa to e	Km11
Hu sa ta shin ka	Hm14
Hum pa hu	Qm4,Qm5
Hum pa to ka	Af2,Af3,Af4,
	Af5,Af6,Af7,Af9,Af10,Af11,
	Bf2,Bf3,Bf4,Bf5,Bf6,Bf7
Hun ka ah she	Gm7,Gm8,
	Gm9,Hm10,Jm8,Jm9,Jm10,
	Qm6,Qm7
Hun ka gra she	Hm11

Hun ka hop pe	Km3,Km4,
	Km5,Nm1,Nm2,Pm8,Pm9,
	Pm10,Pm11
Hun ka hop pe, Lucy	Kf6
Hun ka le ka she	Qm16
Hun ka log ny	Gm10,Gm11,
	Gm12
Hun ka me	If2,If3,If4,If5,
	If6,Jf9,Jf10
Hun ka me tsa he	Jf11,Jf12,
	Jf13,Jf14
Hun ka shin ka	Gm13
Hun ka to ka	Dm2
Hun ka tse a ta	Hm13
Hun ka tun ka	Hm12
Hun ka wa tin an ka	Dm3

J

Jackson, Andrew	Qm2
John	Pm12

K

K she she	Gm14
K she she wa ha he	Hm15
K shon ka	Am12
Ka ha sum pa	Mm15
Ka la moie	Rm15
Ka no ho ha	Rm16
Ka scah	Am6,Am7
Ka se	Am8
Ka tse gre lo	Sm13
Ka wa ho tsa	Jm11
Ka wa se	Jm12
Ke he la pa she	Rm17
Ke le kon pe	Am9
Ke moh ho	Im7
Ke no to	Sm14

Moh e gra to	Sm25
Moh e ka shin ka	Im8
Moh e she	Hm17
Moh ha ah gra	Dm6
Moh ha pa	Kf13
Moh ha pe moie	Rm21
Moh ha sop pe	Im9
Moh ha u gre	Mm25
Moh he sapa me tse	Km13
Moh he se	Dm7
Moh he shu tsy	Em4
Moh he wa kon ta	Fm3
Moh ka ha	Fm4,Fm5
Moh ka se	Rm22
Moh ka shu a	Sm26
Moh ka shu tsy	Sm26
Moh ke ha pe	Bm16
Moh lu ha	Em5
Moh sa hoe e	If11
Moh sa no pa e	Mm22
Moh se num pa	Mm23,Mm24
Moh se tsa he	Ff2,Ff3,Mf49,
	Mf50,Mf51,Mf52,Mf53,
	Mf54,Mf55,Pf5,Pf6
Moh she ha moie	Hm19
Moh she scah ke e ka hre	Em6
Moh she ta moie	Hm20
Moh shon ah ke ta	Mm26
Moh shon ah she a	Mm27
Moh shon hun ka	Hm21
Moh shon ka ha	Im10
Moh shon tse e ta	Mf56,
	Mf57,Mf58,Mf59
Moh shon tse se gra	Em7
Moh shon u kon shon	Sm27
Moh son ho e	If9,If10
Moh ta e ha	Hm22
Moh to e	Mm28
Moie kau ka ha ne	Lm1,Km14
(M ends here)	

Ne ka	Pf9
Ne ka ah ke pa no	Qm8
Ne ka ah sa	Sf5,Sf6,Sf7
Ne ka e se walla	Km15
Ne ka hu a	Sm28
Ne ka she tsa le	Qf11
Ne ka she tse la	Qf7
Ne ka to pa	Qm9
Ne ka wa ti an ka	Em8
Ne o pa ku a	Lm2
Ne ope pe	Bf8
Ne shu moie	Rm23
Ne shu tun ka	Rm24
Ne to pa	Bf9
Ne us pa shu tsy	Cm21
Ne walla	Mm29,Mm30,
	Mm31,Mm32,Mm33
No hro she	Km16
No hu tsa le ka	Gm19
No ka ah pa sha ta	Sm29
No ka to ho	Rm25
No kon sa me	Gf22,Hf6
No me tsa he	Ef8,F4,Ff5
No pa a	Dm8
No pa ku a	Km17
No pa moh le	Sm30
No pa walla	Rm26,Sm31
No she tse a	Sm32
No she walla	Bm17
Nom ka scah	Cf2
Nom tah scah	Cf3
Non pa wa kon ta	Fm6
Num pa se	Hm23,Mm34,
	Mm35,Mm36

O

O ho pe	Bm18
O ke sa	Mm37
O ko tse wa sha ko	Qm18

O la ha moie	Km18
O lo ha walla	Mm39
O pa ho moie	Gm22
O pa le a	Rm27
O pa so shin ka	Sm33
O pa sho e	Mm38
O pa stet sy	Qm19
O pa, Andrew	Im11
O sa ke a	Km19

P

Pa ha ka	Fm4
Pa ha pe son tsa	Bf10,Bf11, Bf12,Bf13
Pa hop pe son tsa	Cf4
Pa hu gra sa	Bf14
Pa hu gra she	Cf5
Pa hu ka shon	Hm24
Pa hu le shon	Mf60,Sf8,Sf9
Pa hu scah	Mm47
Pa le wa we ta	Km20
Pa moh she wa gro	If12
Pa ne wa ha pa le	Rm28
Pa pa wa ho	Mm40,Mm41, Mm42,Mm43,Mm44, Mm45,Mm46
Pa se	Qm20
Pa se he	Hf6
Pa se to pa	Sm34,Sm35
Pa she ah tsa	Sm36
Pa she she	Gf23,Gf24,Gf25, Gf26,Gf27,Gf28,Gf29
Pa su tun ka	Rm29
Pa ta he sha ke a	Sm37
Pa tsa moie	Qm10
Pe se	Mm48
Pe she gre nah she	Sm38
Pe she tun ka	Sm39,Sm40

Pe she u la ha	Sm39,Sm40
Po ku ta	Sf10,Sf11,Sf12
Pon ka me	Af23
Pon ka wa ti an ka	Am14
Prat, Charles	Rm30

S

Sa sa ke ta	Rm31
Sa sa moie	Jm11
Scah gra	Hm25
Se ha	Sm11,Sm14,Sm42
Se la tsa ho tsa	Qm21
Sen tsa shin ka	Sm43
Sen tsa so ta	Sm44
Sen tsa wa kon ta	Sm45, Sm46,Sm47,Sm48
Sen tun ka	Sm49
Sha bla scah	Qm22
Sha ka pa he	Gm23,Hm27
Sha ka scah	Gm24,Hm26
Sha ka wa pe	Km21
Sha pa nah she	Sm50
Sha wa pe	Rm32
She lo tsa we tse	Rm33
Shin ka ki he ka	Em9,Jm4
Shin ka wa sa	Gm25,Hm28
Shin ka wa ti an ka	Km22
Sho no su ka	Hm29
Sho tsa	Qm11
Shon bla scah me	Df5,Df6
Shon e ne la	Pm18
Shon ka hre	Rm34
Shon ka moie	Mm49
Shon ka sop pe	Gm26,Hm30
Shon ka tse a	Jm15
Shon ka u ke pa tsa	Rm8
Shon u le stet sy ka	Rm35
Sin tsa le ka	Qm12

Son se gra	Af24,Bf15,	Tsa moh ke u a	Sm14
	Bf16,Bf17,Cf6	Tsa pa shin ka	Sm56
Son tsa kon ha	Bm19	Tsa pa u le ka	Nm4
Son tsa u gra	Km23	Tsa sa tun ka	Sm57
Strike Axe, Dora	Kf1	Tsa sen tsa	Sm58
		Tsa shin ka wa ti an ka	Sm59
T		Tsa son me	Sf23,Sf24
		Tsa to ah moie	Sm60
Ta ha ka ha	Cm22	Tsa to ah shin ka	Sm62
Ta ko moie	Qm23	Tsa to ah tun ka	Sm61
Ta tsa hu a	Jm16	Tsa to ha	Bm25,Cm24
Ta tsa ko a	Dm9	Tsa to ka	Sm63
Ta tsa to	Dm10	Tsa to ka en tsa	Nm5
Tah ha ha ka	Cm23	Tsa wa hu	Km24
Tah ha ka he	Bm21	Tse moie	Mm54
Tah ha ka wa	Gm8	Tsi shu ah ke pa	Am15,Am16
Tah se a	Bm20	Tsi shu hun ka	Mm55
Tah she ka	Bm22	Tsi shu ki he ka	Mm56
To e ka she	Pm19	Tsi shu shin ka	Mm57,Mm58
To ho ho a	Bm23,Bm24	Tsi shu wa ti an ka	Mm24
To le ho tsa	Mm50		
To op pe	Df7,Pf10,Sf13,	**U**	
	Sf14,Sf15		
To pa moh le	Sm51,Sm52	U hun ka u shon	Lm3
To pa tse	Sm53	U ka ha ha pa	Sm64
To ta ah sa	Rf12,Rf13,Rf14	U ka se tsa	Hm31
To to gre nah she	Qm24	U ka shon	Hm32
To to pa	Df8,Df9	U ke pa to	Sm65
To tsa ah she	Fm7	U ko tse nah she	Sm66
To won e he	Mm51,Mm52	U la ka pe	Sm67
To won ka ha	Mm53	U le ka nah she	Hm33
To won ka she	Rm36	U le sho moie	Hm34
Tsa e kon la	Sf16	U lo ka a	Am17
Tsa hun ka me	Sf17	U me she	Sm68
Tsa le tse	Sm54	U pa she a	Dm11
Tsa me hre	Sf18	U tsa ta wa ha	Am18
Tsa me hun ka	Sf19		
Tsa me se	Sf20,Sf21,Sf22	**W**	
Tsa me tsa he	Of1		
Tsa moh ke le	Sm55	Wa e nah she	Km25

Wa ha ha ta	Qm25	Wa sa op pe	Mf63
Wa ha ka tsa	Am19	Wa sa to shin ka	Mm70,Mm71
Wa ho ho	Gm27,Gm28,Hm36	Wa se se ta	Am20,Am21
Wa ho pa shin ka	Rm37	Wa sha a no pa en	Bm27,Bm28
Wa hra to pa	Pf11,Qf12	Wa sha ah ke pa	Nm7,Pm20
Wa hre hro hro me	Kf24	Wa sha he e	Mf64,Mf65
Wa hre lum pa	Kf16,Kf17,	Wa sha hun ka	Bm29,Bm30,
Kf18,Kf19,Kf20,Kf21,Kf22,			Bm31
	Kf23,Lf3	Wa sha no pa en	Bm25
Wa hre she	Fm8	Wa sha she	Bm32
Wa hu ka hre	Rm38	Wa sha she ah ke pa	Km26
Wa hu la shu	Lm4	Wa sha she me	Kf32
Wa hu son e	Jf15,Jf16,Jf17	Wa sha she me tsa he	Bf19,
Wa ka lum pa	Cf7	Bf20,Bf21,Bf22,Bf23,Bf24,	
Wa ke ah ha ka	Hm6	Bf25,Kf31	
Wa ko ki he ka	Kf25,Mf61,	Wa she ha	Em11
	Mf62	Wa she pe she	Hm37
Wa ko la	Gm29	Wa she sha to ka	Qm26
Wa ko sa moie	Kf26	Wa she u tse	Dm13
Wa kon la tun ka	Gm30,Hm35	Wa shin e se walla	Hm37
Wa kon sa moie	Af25,Af26,	Wa shin ka he	Mm73
Af27,Af28,Af29,Af30,Af31,		Wa shin ka log ny	Pm21
Af32,Af33,Af34,Bf18		Wa shion ka sop pe	Mm72
Wa kon se	Cf8	Wa shin ne ka	Rm40
Wa kon ta e a	Mm59,Mm60,	Wa shin pa	Gm33,Gm34,
Mm61,Mm62,Mm63			Hm38
Wa kon ta he lum pa	Kf27,	Wa shin she a	Hm39
Kf28,Kf29,Kf30		Wa shin wa ha	Am13,Am22,
Wa kon ta pa e	Lm5		Am23
Wa kon tse a	Bm26	Wa sho she	Gm35,Gm36,
Wa le gro le ha	Mm64		Hm40
Wa lo ha ka	Mm65	Wa shon ke la	Pm22
Wa lo ta sa	Rm39	Wa sop a shin ka	Qm28
Wa lu tsa ka she	Fm9	Wa sop a wa kon ta ke	Qm27
Wa na she shin ka	Gm31	Wa sop pe me	Mf66,Qf8
Wa nah she shin ka	Gm32	Wa sop pe wa ko	Ef9
Wa ne a to	Mm66,Mm67,	Wa stat a to	Am24
Mm68,Mm69		Wa stet sy a to	Km28,Mm74,
Wa no ka	Sm69	Mm75,Mm76,Mm77,Mm78,	
Wa no pa she	Dm12	Mm79,Mm80,Mm81,Mm82,	

	Mm83,Mm84,Mm85
Wa stet sy ha	Sm71
Wa to e ke le	Sm19
Wa to e sa	Af35,Af36,Af37,
Af38,Af39,Af40,Af41,Af42	
Wa to e sa a	Bf26
Wa to ka	Nm8
Wa ton	Km27
Wa tsa he to op pe	Gm29
Wa tsa ka wa	Em10
Wa tsa kon la	Km29
Wa tsa me	Df10,Ff6,Pf12
Wa tsa moie	Am24,Am27,
	Am28,Em11

Wa tse ah ha	Am25
Wa tse ki he ka	Am26
Wa tse moie	Am29,Am30
Wa tse tun ka	Am31
Wa tse u he she	Rf15
Wa u we se	Sm72
Wah stah to a	Am24
Ware, Daisy	Mf5
We gra ka ha	Km23
We ha	Af43
We she u ke pe	Sm70
We sop pe she	Qm13
We tse	Km30
We to ha en ka	Rm41

INDEX FOR TRANSLATED NAMES BY CLAN

[Indexed In English]

USER NOTE: Each listed clan is headed by an alphabetical letter such as Clan A, Clan B, etc., through Clan S. All index numbers start with a capital letter which refers to the clan letter. The list is numbered sequentially under Male and under Female headings. To direct the user to a male or female number, a small "m" or small "f" is used after the capital letter. This is followed by an arabic number which refers to the numbered names in the male or female list. Thus, Fm1 would direct the user to Clan F or E gro ka clan, and the male list, number 1 which is Dark Eyes. Likewise, Cf8 would refer the user to Clan C or Ho e ne ka she ka clan, female list, number 8 or Small Animal.

Famed	Sm67	Good Eagle	Gm10
Fear Inspiring	Rm26,Sm31	Good Eagle Woman	Af1,Kf3,
Feathers Blown By The			Lf1,Nf27,Nf1,Pf1
Wind	Hf1	Good Sun	Af22
Fences With The Bow	Cm20	Grass Clings To Him	Sm26
Fire	Dm7	Grass Eater	Sm36
Fire Eyes	Cm3	Gray Heels	Qm21
Fire Walker	Rm10	Great Attacker	Gm30,Hm35
Fish Bone	Cm12	Great Eagle	Hm12
Fish Fins	Cm7	Great Hun Ka	Dm2
Fish Head	Cm9	Greatest In Courage	Am22
Fish Scales	Bm6	Ground Cleared Of Grass	Em5
Fish Skin	Cm6		
Flag Woman	Kf24		
Flames At Every Step	Dm8		
Flashing Eyes	Em3	**H**	
Flat Hands	Qm22		
Flat Wood Woman	Df5	Hair Like Badger's	Qm15
Footprints In The Forest	Af24	Hairy Head	Hm24,Sm37
Footprints In The Woods	Bf15	Handsome Chief	Cm14
Forked Tail Kite	Jf4	Hard To Catch	Hm16
Forked Tail Kite Woman	Jf6	Hated Bird	Hm37
For Whom Arrows Are		Hated Man	Km15
Made	Bm16	Hawk Maker	Pm4
Four Hills	Sm34	Hawk Mena The Favorite	Rf3,
Four Lodges	Hm2		Rf8
Four Wings	Df1	Hawk Passing By	Rm9
Frequenter Of Bushes	Cf4·	Hawk Woman	Cf1,Mf14,Rf7
		He Who Is Called Hun Ka	Km3
G		He Who Is Called Sacred	Km3
		He Who Met The Tsi	
Gazed Upon	Sf13	Shu	Am15
Generous	Fm8	He Who Wins War	
Giver Of Life	Mm29,Mm66	Honors	Em11
Giver Of Speech	Im1	Head Cutter	Mm40
God Who Appears	Kf27	Head Them Off	Sm5
Good Bird	Pm21	Here Are The Footprints	Cf6
Good Chief	Bm13,Cm14	Holes In The Wings	Gm3,Hm1
Good Doctor	Am24,Km28,	Hun Ka Mena The	
	Mm74	Favored	Jf11

O

P

(P ends here)

R

S

T

T (cont.)

The Wanderer	Hm32
Thunder Fear	Rm26,Sm31
Tied Together	Pm6
Town Maker	Mm53
Track On The Prairies	Em7
Tracks Far Away	Am10
Tramples The Grass	Km16
Travels In Distant Lands	Cm18
Travels Over The Land	Mm27
Traveling Cloud	Rm21
Traveling Night	Qm1
Traveling Rain	Rm23
Tree Killer	Rm34
Tree Splitter	Rm35
Trench Full	Sm70
Trots As He Travels	Jm11
Tsi Shu Chief	Mm56
Twinkles	Gm27
Two Crows	Mm15
Two Flags	Kf16,Lf3,Pf11,Qf12
Two Men	Qm9
Two Standards	Kf16,Lf3,Pf11,Qf12
Two Walking	Sm30

V

Valorous	Gm35
Village Maker	Mm53

W

Wa Sha She Me Na The Favorite	Kf31
Wa Sha She Sacred Sun	Bf19
Wa Sha She Woman	Kf32

W (cont.)

Walk By Fours	Sm51
Walking Bull	Sm60
Walking Dog	Mm49
Walking Within	Gm22
Walks Among Cedars	Qm3
Walks As In Fire	Qm23
Walks Home	Sm25
Walks In Death	Mm54
Walks Outside	Sm2
Wanderer	Sm27
Wanders Far Away	Bm10
War Club	Km30
Watches Over The Land	Mm26
Wearer Of Buffalo Hair Head Band	Gm26
Wet Moccasins	Af2,Bf2
Whistle	Jm13
White Back	Cf2
White Bones Woman	Jf15
White Buffalo Woman	Sf23
White Ears	Cf3
White Fish	Bm11,Cm10
White Hair	Mm47
White Hawk Woman	Rf2
White Horn Walks	Cm4
White Horns	Im2
White Plumes	Hm25
White Sun	Ef6,Gf10,Hf5
White Talons	Gm24,Gm26
White Wings	Gm1
Wind Is From The South	Jm2
Winner Of The Race Against The U Tsa Ta	Am18
Wolf Robe	Sm7
Woman Chief	Kf25,Mf61
Woman Of The Night	Qf2
Wriggling Fish	Bm8

OSAGE INDIAN KINSHIP TERMS

This list of Osage kinship terms was collected by P.E. Elder, Osage Agent, in 1862 and published by Lewis H. Morgan in 1870. Since Morgan used English phonics, we did not change his Osage terms into the American phonics of the Annuity Rolls. His pronunciation key precedes the list.

Morgan's kinship terms differ little from those in use during the 1950's. However, some terms, of this earlier period, have been altered through the influence of other tribes. The greatest variation of terms is in the use of the "little mother" term [in nah shin ka]. In 1862, the mother's brother's daughters were called in nah[mother] by the Osages. However, the other Dhegiha Sioux used the "little mother" term consistently from 1862 to the present. The Osage Annuity Rolls never used the "little mother" term although "mother" was sometimes used when the "mother" was younger than the male head of the household. This indicates the mother's brother's daughter was the designated "mother".

These kinship terms must be kept in mind when searching Osage literature. The Jesuits did not leave many clues about their use of son and daughter terms. In all probability, they followed European custom in their use of these terms. Several factors indicate the Annuity Rolls followed Osage custom in the use of kinship terms. A primary factor is the total absence of the European "cousin" term in the full blood listings. Among the mixed bloods, cousin appears frequently on the Rolls.

Two systems of kinship terms can be confusing in research. Any literature involving Osage kinship must be carefully examined to determine the basis of kinship terms used. If it is based on the European system, the task is easy; if the Osage system is the basis, the task is more demanding. The chart of Osage kinship terms becomes especially valuable under these conditions.

Entries in the chart are given in six columns. Headings on the last four columns are self-explanatory. Only the first two headings require some additional explanation. In the first column, the numbers are for indexing purposes. There are four indexes at the end of the chart, one for each of the last four columns. Each of these indexes use the reference numbers in column one. Thus, a reference to 129 would direct the user to sister-in-law, we-hun' ka, my sister-in-law, my wife's sister. The second column, headed M. No., gives Lewis H. Morgan's original number for the term. This was retained for those who wish to pursue an in-depth study of Osage intra and inter-relationships. The indexes should facilitate such studies since Morgan's original list is not indexed.

Four large categories of terms are made. These are: General Kinship Terms, Cousin Terms, In-law Terms, and Step Terms. Terms in each category are then classed by paternity or maternity, comparative age, and sex of the speaker. Since these are factors affecting the term used, it is vital to understand the status between the speaker and the kin.

Both naming practices and kinship terms yield information about a culture. Certainly, Western Civilization differed from Osage Civilization. This is evident from the kinship terms alone. An inquiring mind would immediately notice the absence of cousin from the Osage list of terms. There is no word for cousin in the Osage language. This fact leads to another observation, terms on the maternal side of a family do not correspond with terms on the paternal side. We are then led to observe the mother's brother's daughter is called mother and her children are called brother and sister.

In this way, we are led to conclude that marriages between a man and his brother-in-law's daughter were commonplace events. My mother's sister is not called aunt, she too is called mother and her children are called brother and sister. This, in a like manner, leads to a similar conclusion; a man often married sisters. In fact, both of these conclusions are correct. An Osage man customarily married as many sisters as he could afford. In later life, he would often marry the daughter of his wife's brother.

No sooner do we reach these conclusions, than a host of questions comes to mind. If a man marries several women, there must be some reason for the custom. In addition, multiple marriages of one sex suggests a greater number of that sex than the opposite sex in the culture. Examination of the records does show a ratio of over two females for each male in the Osage tribe. We are led to the question, What caused the imbalance between male and female Osages? A look at the male and female names gives us a clue. Male names reflect war, the hunt, and adventure. Female names are few in number and reflect the peaceful rhythm of life. These roles are verified in the written accounts of Osage life. Males were killed more frequently than females, they died younger. The Annuity Rolls also show a higher infant mortality for males than for females.

Research is a journey without an end. Every answer raises a new set of questions. These lead to more questions and new answers. The more a searching mind discovers, the more it finds unknown. No researcher reaches the end of the journey. The seeking is a goal, not the end.

LEWIS H. MORGAN'S
PRONUNCIATION KEY

VOWELS

a as a in ale, mate.
ä as a in art, father.
ă as a in at, tank.
ạ as a in all, fall.
e as e in even, mete.
ĕ as e in enter, met.
ê has a nasal sound as the French
   en in mien.

i as i in idea, mite.
ĭ as i in it, pity.
o as o in over, go.
ŏ as o in otter, got.
u as u in use, mute.
ŭ as "oo" in food.

CONSONANTS

ch as ch in chin.
g hard as in go.
ğ soft as in gem.
h· represents a deep sonant guttural.
h' represents a breathing sound of
   letter.
kw' represents the same.
ṇ nasal as n in drink.
n' nasal pronounced with the tongue
   pressing the roof of the mouth.
r pronounced with the tip of the
   tongue touching the roof of the
   mouth.

ṣ hissing sound of s.
' An apostrophe after a word denotes
   an almost inaudible breathing
   sound of the last letter.
? An interrogation mark at the end
   of a term implies a doubt of its
   correctness.
A circumflex connecting two syllables indicates that the two are
   pronounced quickly with one
   effort of the voice.

OSAGE INDIAN KINSHIP TERMS

General Kinship Terms

These general terms do not depend on the speaker's sex or age, nor do they depend on the paternity or maternity of the speaker.

No.	M. No.	English Term	Osage Term	Interpretation	Kinship Description
1	1	gt gt grandfather	we-che'-cho	my grandfather	my gt grandfather's father
2	2	gt gt grandmother	e-che'	my grandmother	my gt grandfather's mother
3	3	gt grandfather	we-che'-cho	my grandfather	my gt grandfather
4	4	gt grandmother	e-che'	my grandmother	my gt grandmother
5	5	grandfather	we-che'-cho	my grandfather	my grandfather
6	6	grandmother	e-che'	my grandmother	my grandmother
7	7	father	in-tä'-che	my father	my father
8	229	husband	ne-cha'	my husband	my husband
9	8	mother	in-nah'	my mother	my mother

10	230	wife	wa-che'	my wife	my wife
11	9	son	we-she'-kä	my son	my son
12	25-26	brothers	we-she'-lä	my brothers	my brothers
13	10	daughter	we-shon'-ka	my daughter	my daughter
14	27-28	sisters	we-tun'-ka	my sisters	my sisters
15	11	grandson	we-chose'-pä	my grandchild	my grandson
16	12	granddaughter	we-chose'-pä	my grandchild	my granddaughter
17	13	gt grandson	we-chose'-pä	my grandchild	my gt grandson
18	14	gt granddaughter	we-chose'-pä	my grandchild	my gt granddaughter
19	15	gt gt grandson	we-chose'-pä	my grandchild	my gt grandson's son
20	16	gt gt granddaughter	we-chose'-pä	my grandchild	my gt grandson's daughter
21	33-49	gr nephew	we-chose'-pä	my grandchild	my brother's grandson
22	34-50	gr niece	we-chose'-pä	my grandchild	my brother's granddaughter
23	35-51	gt gr nephew	we-chose'-pä	my grandchild	my brother's gt grandson

24	36-52	gt gr niece	we-chose'-pä	my grandchild	my brother's gt granddaughter
25	41-57	gr nephew	we-chose'-pä	my grandchild	my sister's grandson
26	42-58	gr niece	we-chose'-pä	my grandchild	my sister's granddaughter
27	43-59	gt gr nephew	we-chose'-pä	my grandchild	my sister's gt grandson
28	44-60	gt gr niece	we-chose'-pä	my grandchild	my sister's gt granddaughter
29	266	widow	wä-cho-ne-ka-ket-so	widow	widow
30	267	widower	ne-ko-no-cho-ket-so	widower	widower
31	268	twins	no-po'-tä	twins	twins

These general terms do not depend on the speaker's sex or age, however, they depend on the paternity or maternity of the speaker.

32	61	paternal uncle	in-tä'-che	my father	my father's brother
33	113	maternal uncle	we-ja'-ga	my uncle	my mother's brother
34	87	paternal aunt	we-je'-me	my aunt	my father's sister

35	139	maternal aunt	in-nah'	my mother	my mother's sister
36	165	paternal gt uncle	we-che'-cho	my grandfather	my father's father's brother
37	185	maternal gt uncle	we-che'-cho	my grandfather	my mother's mother's brother
38	175	paternal gt aunt	e-che'	my grandmother	my father's father's sister
39	195	maternal gt aunt	e-che'	my grandmother	my mother's mother's sister
40	205	paternal gt gt uncle	we-che'-cho	my grandfather	my father's father's father's brother
41	217	maternal gt gt uncle	we-che'-cho	my grandfather	my mother's mother's mother's brother
42	211	paternal gt gt aunt	e-che'	my grandmother	my father's father's father's sister
43	223	maternal gt gt aunt	e-che'	my grandmother	my mother's mother's mother's sister

These general terms do not depend on the speaker's age, paternity, or maternity, however, they do depend on the sex of the speaker.

| 44 | 29 | nephew [male speaking] | we-shen'-kä | my son | my brother's son |
| 45 | 45 | nephew [female speaking] | we-chose'-kä | my nephew | my brother's son |

117

46	31	niece [male speaking]	we-shon'-ka	my daughter	my brother's daughter
47	47	niece [female speaking]	we-che'-zho	my niece	my brother's daughter
48	37	nephew [male speaking]	we-chose'-kä	my nephew	my sister's son
49	53	nephew [female speaking]	we-shen'-kä	my son	my sister's son
50	39	niece [male speaking]	we-che'-zho	my niece	my sister's daughter
51	55	niece [female speaking]	we-shon'-ka	my daughter	my sister's daughter

These general terms do not depend on paternity or maternity of the speaker, however, they do depend on the sex of the speaker and the age difference between the kin and the speaker.

52	17	[older] brother [male speaking]	we-she'-lä	my elder brother	my elder brother
53	18	[older] brother [female speaking]	we-chin'-to	my elder brother	my elder brother
54	19	[older] sister [male speaking]	we-tun'-ka	my elder sister	my elder sister

118

55	20	[older] sister [female speaking]	we-sho'-la	my elder sister	my elder sister

These general terms do not depend on the sex, paternity, or maternity of the speaker, however, they do depend on the age difference between the kin and the speaker.

56	21-22	[younger] brother	we-son'-kä	my younger brother	my younger brother
57	23-24	[younger] sister	we-tun'-ka	my younger sister	my younger sister

119

Cousin Terms

These cousin terms do not depend on the sex or age of the speaker, however, they do depend on the paternity and maternity of the speaker.

No.	M. No.	English Term	Osage Term	Interpretation	Kinship Description
58	77-78	paternal 2nd cousin	we-shon'-ka	my daughter	my father's brother's son's daughter
59	129-130	maternal 2nd cousin	in-nah'	my mother	my mother's brother's son's daughter
60	83	paternal 3rd cousin	we-chose'-pä	my grandchild	my father's brother's gt grandson
61	135	maternal 3rd cousin	we-ja'-ga	my uncle	my mother's brother's gt grandson
62	109	paternal 3rd cousin	we-chose'-pä	my grandchild	my father's sister's gt grandson
63	161	maternal 3rd cousin	we-chose'-pä	my grandchild	my mother's sister's gt grandson
64	84	paternal 3rd cousin	we-chose'-pä	my grandchild	my father's brother's gt granddaughter
65	136	maternal 3rd cousin	we-che'-zho	my niece	my mother's brother's gt granddaughter

66	110	paternal 3rd cousin	we-chose'-pä	my grandchild	my father's sister's gt granddaughter
67	162	maternal 3rd cousin	we-chose'-pä	my grandchild	my mother's sister's gt granddaughter
68	85	paternal 4th cousin	we-chose'-pä	my grandchild	my father's brother's gt grandson's son
69	137	maternal 4th cousin	we-ja'-ga	my uncle	my mother's brother's gt grandson's son
70	86	paternal 4th cousin	we-chose'-pä	my grandchild	my father's brother's gt grandson's daughter
71	138	maternal 4th cousin	we-chose'-pä	my grandchild	my mother's brother's gt grandson's daughter
72	111	paternal 4th cousin	we-chose'-pä	my grandchild	my father's sister's gt grandson's son
73	163	maternal 4th cousin	we-chose'-pä	my grandchild	my mother's sister's gt grandson's son
74	112	paternal 4th cousin	we-chose'-pä	my grandchild	my father's sister's gt grandson's daughter

75	164	maternal 4th cousin	we-chose'-pä	my grandchild	my mother's sister's gt granddaughter's daughter
76	101-102	paternal 2nd cousin	we-chose'-pä	my grandchild	my father's sister's son's son
77	127-128	maternal 2nd cousin	we-ja'-ga	my uncle	my mother's brother's son's son
78	103-104	paternal 2nd cousin	we-chose'-pä	my grandchild	my father's sister's son's daughter
79	105-106	paternal 2nd cousin	we-chose'-pä	my grandchild	my father's sister's daughter's son
80	107-108	paternal 2nd cousin	we-chose'-pä	my grandchild	my father's sister's daughter's daughter

These cousin terms do not depend on the relative age of the speaker, however, they do depend on the sex, paternity, and maternity of the speaker.

81	75	paternal 2nd cousin [male speaking]	we-shen'-ka	my son	my father's brother's son's son
82	76	paternal 2nd cousin [female speaking]	we-shen'-ka	my nephew	my father's brother's son's son

122

83	153	maternal 2nd cousin [male speaking]	my son	we-she'-ka	my mother's sister's son's son
84	154	maternal 2nd cousin [female speaking]	my nephew	we-chose'-kä	my mother's sister's son's son
85	79	paternal 2nd cousin [male speaking]	my nephew	we-chose'-kä	my father's brother's daughter's son
86	80	paternal 2nd cousin [female speaking]	my son	we-shon'-kä	my father's brother's daughter's son
87	131	maternal 2nd cousin [male speaking]	my elder brother	we-she'-lä	my mother's brother's daughter's son
88	132	maternal 2nd cousin [female speaking]	my elder brother	we-chin'-to	my mother's brother's daughter's son
89	81	paternal 2nd cousin [male speaking]	my niece	we-chose'-ka	my father's brother's daughter's daughter
90	82	paternal 2nd cousin [female speaking]	my daughter	we-shon'-ka	my father's brother's daughter's daughter
91	133	maternal 2nd cousin [male speaking]	my elder sister	we-tun'-ka	my mother's brother's daughter's daughter

92	134	maternal 2nd cousin [female speaking]	we-sho'-la	my elder sister	my mother's brother's daughter's daughter
93	155	maternal 2nd cousin [male speaking]	we-shon'-ka	my daughter	my mother's sister's son's daughter
94	156	maternal 2nd cousin [female speaking]	we-che'-zho	my niece	my mother's sister's son's daughter
95	157	maternal 2nd cousin [male speaking]	we-chose'-kä	my nephew	my mother's sister's daughter's son
96	158	maternal 2nd cousin [female speaking]	we-shen'-kä	my son	my mother's sister's daughter's son
97	159	maternal 2nd cousin [male speaking]	we-che'-zho	my niece	my mother's sister's daughter's daughter
98	160	maternal 2nd cousin [female speaking]	we-shon'-ka	my daughter	my mother's sister's daughter's daughter

These cousin terms depend on the sex, paternity, maternity, and age difference between the kin and the speaker.

| 99 | 63 | paternal [older] cousin [male speaking] | we-she'-lä | my elder brother | my father's brother's son – older than myself |

100	64	paternal [older] cousin [female speaking]	we-chin'-to	my elder brother	my father's brother's son – older than myself
101	69	paternal [older] cousin [male speaking]	we-tun-ka	my elder sister	my father's brother's daughter – older than myself
102	70	paternal [older] cousin [female speaking]	we-sho'-ka	my elder sister	my father's brother's daughter – older than myself
103	89	paternal [older] cousin [male speaking]	we-chose'-kä	my nephew	my father's sister's son – older than myself
104	90	paternal [older] cousin [female speaking]	we-shen'-kä	my son	my father's sister's son – older than myself
105	141	maternal [older] cousin [male speaking]	we-she'-lä	my elder brother	my mother's sister's son – older than myself
106	142	maternal [older] cousin [female speaking]	we-chin'-to	my elder brother	my mother's sister's son – older than myself
107	91	paternal [younger] cousin [male speaking]	we-chose'-kä	my nephew	my father's sister's son – younger than myself
108	92	paternal [younger] cousin [female speaking]	we-shen'-kä	my son·	my father's sister's son – younger than myself

109	95	paternal [older] cousin [male speaking]	we-che'-zho	my niece	my father's sister's daughter – older than myself
110	96	paternal [older] cousin [female speaking]	we-shon'-ka	my daughter	my father's sister's daughter – older than myself
111	147	maternal [older] cousin [male speaking]	we-tun'-ka	my elder sister	my mother's sister's daughter – older than myself
112	148	maternal [older] cousin [female speaking]	we-sho'-la	my elder sister	my mother's sister's daughter – older than myself
113	97	paternal [younger] cousin [male speaking]	we-che'-zho	my niece	my father's sister's daughter – younger than myself
114	98	paternal [younger] cousin [female speaking]	we-shon'-ka	my daughter	my father's sister's daughter – younger than myself

These cousin terms do not depend on the sex of the speaker, however, they do depend on the paternity, maternity, and age difference between the kin and the speaker.

115	115-116	maternal [older] cousin	we-ja'-ga	my uncle	my mother's brother's son – older than myself
116	65-66	paternal [younger] cousin	we-son'-kä	my younger brother	my father's brother's son – younger than myself

117	117-118	maternal [younger] cousin	be-ja'-ga	my uncle	my mother's brother's son – younger than myself
118	71-72	paternal [younger] cousin	we-tun'-ka	my younger sister	my father's brother's daughter – younger than myself
119	121-122	maternal [older] cousin	in-nah'	my mother	my mother's brother's daughter – older than myself
120	123-124	maternal [younger] cousin	in-nah'	my mother	my mother's brother's daughter – younger than myself
121	143-144	maternal [younger] cousin	we-son'-kä	my younger brother	my mother's sister's son – younger than myself
122	149-150	maternal [younger] cousin	we-tun'-ka	my younger sister	my mother's sister's daughter – younger than myself

127

In-law Terms

These in-law terms do not depend on the sex, paternity, maternity,
or age difference between the kin and the speaker.

No.	M. No.	English Term	Osage Term	Interpretation	Kinship Description
123	231	father-in-law	we-che'-cho	my grandfather	my husband's father
124	232	mother-in-law	e-che'	my grandmother	my husband's mother
125	233	grandfather-in-law	we-che'-cho	my grandfather	my husband's grandfather
126	234	grandmother-in-law	e-che'	my grandmother	my husband's grandmother
127	254	brother-in-law	we-she'-kä	my brother-in-law	my husband's brother
128	257	brother-in-law	we-tä'-ha	my brother-in-law	my wife's brother
129	260	sister-in-law	we-hun'-kä	my sister-in-law	my wife's sister
130	261	sister-in-law	we-she'-kä	my sister-in-law	my husband's sister
131	32-48	nephew-in-law	we-ton'-chä	my son-in-law	my brother's daughter's husband
132	30-46	niece-in-law	we-che'-ne	my daughter-in-law	my brother's brother's son's wife

133	40-56	nephew-in-law	we-ton'-chä	my son-in-law	my sister's daughter's husband
134	38-54	niece-in-law	we-che'-ne	my daughter-in-law	my sister's son's wife
135	239-240	son-in-law	we-ton'-chä	my son-in-law	my son-in-law
136	241-242	daughter-in-law	we-che'-ne	my daughter-in-law	my daughter-in-law

These in-law terms do not depend on the sex or age difference between the kin and the speaker, however, they do depend on the paternity and maternity of the speaker.

137	88	paternal uncle-in-law	we-tä'-he	my brother-in-law	my father's sister's husband
138	140	maternal uncle-in-law	in-tä'-che [some ?]	my father [some ?]*	my mother's sister's husband

* Morgan indicated he was theorizing about this term. Possibly confusion arose because often one man married all the sisters in a family. Thus, the mother's sisters were mother to all the children of that union. This would make one man, father-in-fact, of all the children. Confusion could arise when sisters married different men.

139	62	paternal aunt-in-law	in-nä'	my mother	my father's brother's wife
140	114	maternal aunt-in-law	we-je'-me	my aunt	my mother's brother's wife
141	99-100	paternal cousin-in-law	we-ton'-chä	my son-in-law	my father's sister's daughter's husband

142	93-94	paternal cousin-in-law	we-che'-ne	my daughter-in-law	my father's sister's son's wife
143	125-126	maternal cousin-in-law	in-tä'-che	my father	my mother's brother's daughter's

These in-law terms do not depend on the paternity, maternity, or age difference between the kin and the speaker, however, they do depend on the sex of the speaker.

144	255	brother-in-law [male speaking]	we-tä'-ha	my brother-in-law	my sister's husband
145	256	brother-in-law [female speaking]	we-she'-kä	my brother-in-law	my sister's husband
146	262	sister-in-law [male speaking]	we-hun'-kä	my sister-in-law	my brother's wife
147	263	sister-in-law [female speaking]	we-she'-kä	my sister-in-law	my brother's wife

These in-law terms do not depend on the relative age of the speaker, however, they do depend on the sex, paternity, and maternity of the speaker.

148	67	paternal cousin-in-law [male speaking]	we-hun'-kä	my sister-in-law	my father's brother's son's wife

149	68	paternal cousin-in-law [female speaking]	we-she'-kä	my sister-in-law	my father's brother's son's wife
150	119	maternal cousin-in-law [male speaking]	be-je'-me	my aunt	my mother's brother's son's wife
151	120	maternal cousin-in-law [female speaking]	we-je'-me	my aunt	my mother's brother's son's wife
152	73	paternal cousin-in-law [male speaking]	we-tä'-ha	my brother-in-law	my father's brother's daughter's husband
153	74	paternal cousin-in-law [female speaking]	we-she'-kä	my brother-in-law	my father's brother's daughter's husband
154	145	maternal cousin-in-law [male speaking]	we-hun'-kä	my sister-in-law	my mother's sister's son's wife
155	146	maternal cousin-in-law [female speaking]	we-she'-kä	my sister-in-law	my mother's sister's son's wife
156	151	maternal cousin-in-law [male speaking]	we-tä'-ha	my brother-in-law	my mother's sister's daughter's husband
157	152	maternal cousin-in-law [female speaking]	we-she'-kä	my brother-in-law	my mother's sister's daughter's husband

131

Step Terms

These step terms do not depend on sex, age, paternity, or maternity of the speaker.

No.	M. No.	English Term	Osage Term	Translation	Kinship Description
158	243	step-father	in-tä'-che	my father	my step-father
159	244	step-mother	in-nah'	my mother	my step-mother
160	245-246	step-son	we-she'-kä	my son	my step-son
161	247	step-daughter	we-shoṇ'-ka	my daughter	my step-daughter

The step terms do not depend on the speaker's paternity or maternity, however, they do depend on the sex and age difference between the kin and the speaker.

| 162 | 248 | [older] step-brother [male speaking] | we-she'-lä | my elder brother | my step-brother |
| 163 | 249 | [older] step-brother [female speaking] | we-chiṇ'-to | my elder brother | my step-brother |

132

164	250	[older] step-sister [male speaking]	we-tun'-ka	my elder sister	my step-sister
165	251	[older] step-sister [female speaking]	we-sho'-la	my elder sister	my step-sister
		These step terms do not depend on the speaker's sex, paternity, or maternity, however, they do depend on the age difference between the kin and the speaker.			
166	248-249	[younger] step-brother	we-son'-kä	my younger brother	my step-brother
167	250-251	[younger] step-sister	we-tun'-ka	my younger sister	my step-sister

133

OSAGE INDIAN KINSHIP TERMS

INDEX

Index Of English Terms

B

D

F

G

H

M

N

O

O (cont.)

P

S

S (cont.)

T

W

Y

Index Of Osage Terms

B

E

I

N

W

138

W (cont.)

139

Index Of Translated Terms

A

B

D

E

E (cont.)

F

G

H

M

N

S

T

U

W

Y

Index Of Kinship Descriptions

B

D

E

F

F (cont.)

G

H

M

146

M (cont.)

S

S (cont.)

T

W

Y

OSAGE INDIAN SYLLABLES

An unwritten language always presents a problem for literate people. Osage is an oral language which has been written many ways. Pronunciation keys give sounds for individual letters, but syllable sounds often give more accurate sounds than individual letters. In some cases, Osage syllables are spellings of single letter sounds, in other instances they are sounds of several letters in combination. Various peoples have attempted to write Osage words with the phonics to which they were accustomed. The result is a myriad assortment of spellings.

The French were first to put Osage in a written form. Their influence has greatly affected what has been written in Osage. Spanish made few inroads in written Osage. Their records often mention the Osages, but the effect on written Osage was slight. American style English dominates written Osage today. No style of English has the correct sounds for all Osage words. Dr. Francis La Flesche uses a combination of English, French, and German sounds to achieve the Osage speech sounds. The result is an accurate reflection of the Osage language.

It is unfortunate that La Flesche wrote his dictionary too late for everyday use. By the 1920's the Osages were already accustomed to the American style English spellings for their language. We admire and deeply respect La Flesche for his efforts to preserve an accurate reflection of the Osage language in a written form. The same esteem is held for John J. Mathews, who wrote in La Flesche's phonics. However, we are aware that few Americans and fewer Osages, can easily decipher La Flesche's system of sounds.

Aside from La Flesche's work with the Smithsonian and John J. Mathews', *The Osages,* no other significant sources of Osage information uses La Flesche's system. Yet, La Flesche left us a great gift in his dictionary. Most osages have a scant vocabulary in the Osage language. Osage and non-Osage alike will find his dictionary a necessity in Osage research. We have attempted to ease the problems arising from written Osage with a syllable conversion table.

No claim of extreme accuracy or completeness is made for the table. It is intended as a rough guide for written Osage words. Many Osage words refer to events from legends or to things of the Osage culture and require an Osage culture background for comprehension, if not identification of the word. Few recorders of Osage information had a trained ear for linguistics. Most lacked more than a rudimentary knowledge of phonics. The result is often an incomprehensible string of syllables which seeks to express something in Osage. Under these conditions, the task of bringing extreme accuracy and completeness to any list of syllables becomes prohibitive.

We have taken the American phonics of the Annuity Rolls as our standard of written Osage. This was done, not because it was superior, but because it is the system most widely understood. Francis La Flesche's system of phonics was included because his dictionary gives a core knowledge of the Osage language. Fr. Paul M. Ponziglione's system was included because of the valuable Jesuit records of Osage Mission. We must mention that our sample base of Fr. Ponziglione's sounds was limited to about three hundred words. Therefore, this list is' somewhat defective.

As a convenience to the user three alphabetized tables are included. The first table is alphabetized, in the first column, by the American phonics of the Annuity Rolls. In the second table, Dr. La Flesche's syllables are listed in the first column in alphabetical order. Fr. Ponziglione's syllables are alphabetized first in the last table. This conversion table should enable a researcher to change written Osage to any of the three systems listed. Under ordinary conditions, the meaning can also be obtained from La Flesche's dictionary by converting to his phonics.

CONVERSION TABLE

FOR

OSAGE INDIAN SYLLABLES

Alphabetized By Annuity Roll Syllables

Annuity Rolls	F. La-Flesche	Fr. Ponziglione	Annuity Rolls	F. La-Flesche	Fr. Ponziglione
A			**D**		
a	e	e	da	none	da
a	e	eh	dah	none	da
ah	a	a			
ah	tha	a	**E**		
an	wo^n	han			
ap	a	a	e	i	e
ap pe	a be	ha pe	e	i	eh
ap py	a be	ha pe	e	i	his
			e	i	i
B			e	i^n	his
			ea	none	eh
bla	bthe	none	e'k	none	ich
blah	btha	none	en	i^n	his
blah	bthe	none	en	i^n	in
			e'sah	none	hissa
C			e'sh	none	ich
			estah	shta	none
cha	xtha	none			
che	chi	che	**G**		
che	ts'i^n	chi			
che	xe	chi	g	gi	g
che	xi	che	g	gi	gka
che	xthe	chi	gah	ga	ga
che	xthi	che	gah heh	gthe	ga he
cho	xo^n	none	gah hre	gthi^n	ga chre
chon	xo^n	chan	gany	gthi^n	none

ge	xthe	gi	hon	ho^n	han
gla	gthe	gra	hon	ho^n	hu
glo	gtho^n	none	hop	a	ha
gra	gthe	gra	hop pe	a be	ha pe
gra	gthe	gre	hop py	a be	ha pe
grah	gtha	gra	hrah	xtha	chre
grah	gtha	gre	hre	xtha	chre
grah	gthe	gra	hre	xthi	chre
grah	gthe	gre	hre	xthi^n	chre
grah	gtho^n	gra	hre ke	xthe	none
grah	gtho^n	gre	hro	xtho^n	none
grah	o^n be	gra	hu	hi^n	hu
grah	o^n be	gre	hu	hiu	hu
gre	gthe	gre	hu	hu	hu
gre	gthi	gri	hu	ki^n	hu
gro	none	kru	hum	ho^n	hum
gru	gthu	kru	hun	ho^n	han
			hun	ho^n	an
	H		hun	ho^n	hu

ha	hi^n	ha		**I**	
ha	xa	ha			
hah	ha	ha	i	e	e
hah	we thi^n	ha	in	i^n	in
hah	xa	ha			
han	none	an		**K**	
han	none	han			
he	he	he	k	none	ch
he	hi	hi	k	none	g
he	hi^n	hin	ka	ga	ca
he	xe	che	ka	ga	k
he	xe	he	ka	ka	ca
he	xi	che	ka	k'a	le
he	xi^n	chi	ka	xthe	cha
heh	xe	hin	ka	xthe	che
hen	xi^n	hin	ka	xthe	chie
ho	ho	hu	ka	xthe	g'ke
ho	ho^n	han	ka	xthe	la
ho	ho^n	ha	ka	xthe	le
ho	ho^n	hu	kah	ga	chie
hon	ho^n	an	kah	ga	ga

	K (cont.)			L (cont.)	
kah	ga	ka	log	tha	none
kah	ga	la	loh	tho	lo
kah	ka	ka	loh	tho	lu
ḳah	ka	le	lum	tho^n	none
kah	k'a	g'ke			
kah	ho^n	cha		**M**	
kah	ho^n	che			
kah	ho^n	gka	ma	ma	ma
kan	none	chan	mah	ma	ma
ke	gi	chie	me	mi	me
ke	ke	le	me	mi	mi
ke	xthe	chi	me	mi	min
ke	xthe	g ki	me	mi	mis
keh	ki^n	chi	me	mi	mint
keh	ki^n	chie	me	mi	mit
keh	ki^n	le	me	wi^n	mi
kea	ge	none	meh	wi^n	min
key	none	chie	meh	wi^n	mint
ki	ga	none	men	wi^n	min
ko	k'o	com	mo	mo^n	man
ko	k'o	con	moh	mo^n	man
ko	k'o	lo	mon	mo^n	ma
ko	k'o	lu			
koh	ko^n	gku		**N**	
koh	ko^n	lo			
koh	ko^n	lu	na	no^n	na
kon	ko^n	chan	na	no^n	nas
kon	ko^n	com	nah	no^n	na
kon	ko^n	con	nah	no^n	nas
			nam	no^n	nam
	L		nam	no^n	nan
			ne	ni	ni
la	the	la	ne	ni	nin
la	the	le	no	hno^n	none
lah	the	la	nom	no^n	nam
lah	the	le	nom	no^n	num
le	thi	le	non	hno^n	nam
le	thi^n	le	non	no^n	num
lo	tho	lo	num	no^n	num
lo	tho	lu	nun	no^n	nam
			nun	no^n	num

o	o	aus	scah	ço^n	scha
o	o	u	se	ç	c
o gla	do ba	none	se	ç	ci
o gla	du ba	none	se	ç	si
o pah	xo^n	none	sea	çi a	shie
op pe	a be	none	se'a	çi a	shie
op py	a be	none	se ka	çi ka	ck
os	none	aus	se kah	çi ka	cke
			sek a tah	none	ckta
P			sen	çi^n	none
			se ne	çne	none
pa	ba	pa	sh	none	ch
pa	pa	pe	sha	çe	che
pah	ba	pe	sha	sha	chai
pah	pa	pa	sha	sha	sha
pe	be	pe	shah	sha	sha
pe	xpe	pe	sha ta	sha ta	chta
pop	ba	none	sha tah	sha ta	chta
pop	bo^n	none	she	zhe	che
pu	bu	none	she	zhi	chi
			she	zhi	she
R			she	zhi	shi
			she	zhi^n	se
ra	the	none	shin	xthi	shin
rah	the	none	shin	zhi^n	shin
			sho	none	shu
S			shon	zho^n	chan
			shon	zho^n	shan
sa	çe	se	shon	zho^n	shu
sa	çi	ze	shon	zho^n	shun
sa	sha	ze	shop	zha	shu
sah	çe	sa	shu	zhiu	shu
sah	çe	se	son	ço^n	san
sah	çe	sans	sop	ça	sa
sah	çe	son	stah	stse	none
sah	çe	ze	stat	stse	none
sah	sha	ze	su	çu	su
scah	çka	scha	sun	none	san

S (cont.)		
sy	none	su

T		
ta	da	da
ta	ṭa	ta
ta	ṭa	te
tah	da	da
tah	da	dra
tah	da	ta
tah	da	taw
tah	da	te
tah	ṭa	tha
tah sah	ṭs'a	di
te	ṭi	di
teh	ṭi	di
te sa	ṭs'a	di se
ti	ṭi	di
tish	ṭsi	tchi
to	ṭo	tu
to	to^n	ta
to e	none	toe
toh	to^n	ta
toh	ṭa	tan
tom	to^n	tan
tom	ṭa	tan
ton	to^n	tan
ton	to^n	ton
tow	to^n	taw
tsa	dse	tce
tsa	ṭse	tshe
tsa	ṭse	tza
tsa	ṭse	tze
tse	dse	tce
tse	dse	tchi
tse	dse	tsde
tse	dse	tse
tse	dse	tsi
tse	ṭsi	tze
tse	ṭs'i^n	tse

T (cont.)		
tse	ṭsi	tssi
tse	ṭse	tzi
tsah	ṭse	tsha
tseh	none	tzie
tshe	none	tchi
tsi	ṭse	tchi
tsi	ṭse	tssi
tsy	dse	tsy
tsy	dse	tsy
tun	to^n	tan
tun	to^n	ton

U		
u	u	u
u	zhu	u
ue	zhu	ui
um	none	on
um	none	um
uz	none	us

W		
wa	wa	soi
wa	wa	we
wah	wa	soi
wah	wa	we
wah	wa	wha
wah	wa	whas
we	wi	sue
we	wi	ui
we	wi	vi
we	wi	we
we	wi	win
we	wi	wue
weh	no^n	we
wo	wo^n	none
woh	wo^n	none
wu	wo^n	none
wu an	xwi^n	none

W (cont.)

wun	wo^n	none

Y

y	none	us
ys	none	us

End of Annuity Rolls Index

CONVERSION TABLE

FOR

OSAGE INDIAN SYLLABLES

Alphabetized By Francis La Flesche's Syllables

F. La-Flesche	Annuity Rolls	Fr. Pon-ziglione	F. La-Flesche	Annuity Rolls	Fr. Pon-ziglione
		A			C (cont.)
a	ah	a	çe	sa	se
a	ap	a	çe	sah	sa
a	hop	ha	çe	sah	se
a be	ap pe	ha pe	çe	sah	sans
a be	ap py	ha pe	çe	sah	son
a be	hop pe	ha pe	çe	sah	ze
a be	hop py	ha pe	çe	sha	che
a be	op pe	ha pe	çi	sa	ze
a be	op py	ha pe	çi a	sea	shie
			çi a	se'a	shie
		B	çi ka	se ka	ck
			çi ka	se kah	cke
ba	pa	pa	çin	sen	none
ba	pah	pe	çka	scah	scha
ba	pop	none	çne	se ne	none
be	pe	pe	çon	scah	scha
bo^n	pop	none	çon	son	san
btha	blah	none	çu	su	su
bthe	bla	none			
bthe	blah	none			D
bu	pu	none			
			da	ta	te
		C	da	tah	da
			da	tah	dra
chi	che	che	da	tah	ta
ç	se	c	da	tah	taw
ç	se	ci	da	tah	te
ç	se	si	do ba	o gla	none
ça	sop	sa	dse	tsa	tce

157

dse	tse	tce
dse	tse	tchi
dse	tse	tsde
dse	tse	tse
dse	tse	tsi
dse	tsy	tsy
dse	tsy	tze
du ba	o gla	none

E

e	a	e
e	a	eh
e	i	e

G

ga	gah	ga
ga	ka	ca
ga	ka	k
ga	kah	chie
ga	kah	ga
ga	kah	ka
ga	kah	la
ga	kah	le
ga	ki	none
ge	kea	none
gi	g	g
gi	g	gka
gi	ke	chie
gtha	grah	gra
gtha	grah	gre
gthe	ga heh	ga he
gthe	gla	gra
gthe	gra	gra
gthe	gra	gre
gthe	grah	gra
gthe	grah	gre
gthe	gre	gre
gthi	gre	gri

$gthi^n$	gah hre	ga chre
$gthi^n$	gany	none
$gtho^n$	glo	none
$gtho^n$	grah	gra
$gtho^n$	grah	gre
gthu	gru	kru

H

ha	hah	ha
he	he	he
hi	he	hi
hi^n	ha	ha
hi^n	he	hin
hi^n	hu	hu
hiu	hu	hu
hno^n	no	none
hno^n	non	nam
ho	ho	hu
ho^n	ho	ho
ho^n	ho	han
ho^n	ho	hu
ho^n	hon	an
ho^n	hon	han
ho^n	hon	hu
ho^n	hum	hum
ho^n	hun	an
ho^n	hun	han
ho^n	hun	hu
hu	hu	hu

I

i	e	e
i	e	eh
i	e	his
i	e	i
i^n	e	his
i^n	en	his
i^n	en	in
i^n	in	in

K

ḳa	ka	ca
k'a	ka	le
k'a	kah	g'ke
ka	kah	ka
ḳe	ke	le
ki^n	hu	hu
ki^n	keh	chi
ki^n	keh	chie
ki^n	keh	le
k'o	ko	com
k'o	ko	con
k'o	ko	lo
k'o	ko	lu
ko^n	kah	cha
ko^n	kah	che
ko^n	kah	gka
ko^n	koh	gku
ko^n	koh	lo
ko^n	koh	lu
ko^n	kon	chan
ko^n	kon	com
ko^n	kon	con

M

ma	ma	ma
ma	mah	ma
mi	me	me
mi	me	mi
mi	me	min
mi	me·	mint
mi	me	mis
mi	me	mit
mo^n	mo	man
mo^n	mon	ma
mo^n	moh	man

N

ni	ne	ni
ni	ne	nin
no^n	na	na
no^n	na	nas
no^n	nah	na
no^n	nah	nas
no^n	nam	nam
no^n	nam	nan
no^n	nom	nam
no^n	nom	num
no^n	non	num
no^n	num	num
no^n	nun	nam
no^n	nun	num

O

o	o	aus
o	o	u
o^n be	grah	gra
o^n be	grah	gre

P

ṗa	pa	pe
ṗa	pah	pa

S

sha	sa	ze
sha	sah	ze
sha	sha	chai
sha	sha	sha
sha	shah	sha
sha ta	sha ta	chta
sha tah	sha ta.	chta

shta	estah	none		ṭse	tsa	tshe
stse	stah	none		ṭse	tsa	tza
stse	stat	none		ṭse	tsa	tze
				ṭse	tsah	tsha
	T			ṭse	tse	tzi
ṭa	ta	da		ṭse	tsi	tchi
ṭa	ta	ta		ṭse	tsi	tssi
ṭa	tah	tha		ṭsi	tish	tchi
ṭa	toh	tan		ṭsi	tse	tssi
ṭa	tom	tan		ṭsi	tse	tze
tha	ah	a		ṭs'i^n	che	chi
tha	log	none		ṭs'i^n	tse	tse
the	la	la				
the	la	le			**U**	
the	lah	la				
the	lah	le		u	u	u
the	ra	none				
the	rah	none			**W**	
thi	le	le				
thi^n	le	le		wa	wa	soi
tho	lo	lo		wa	wa	we
tho	lo	lu		wa	wah	soi
tho	loh	lo		wa	wah	we
tho	loh	lu		wa	wah	wha
thon	lum	none		wa	wab	whas
ṭi	te	di		we th..	bdh	ha
ṭi	teh	di		wi	we	sue
ṭi	ti	di		wi	we	ui
ṭo	to	tu		wi	we	vi
to^n	to	ta		wi	we	we
to^n	toh	ta		wi	we	win
to^n	tom	tan		wi	we	wue
to^n	ton	tan		wi^n	me	mi
to^n	ton	ton		wi^n	ineh	min
to^n	tow	taw		wi^n	meh	mint
to^n	tun	tan		wi^n	men	min
to^n	tun	ton		wo^n	..	han
ṭs'a	tah sah	ta sa		wo^n	wo	none
ts'a	te sa	di se		wo^n	woh	none

CONVERSION TABLE

FOR

OSAGE INDIAN SYLLABLES

Alphabetized By Fr. Ponziglione's Syllables

Fr. Ponziglione	Annuity Rolls	F. La-Flesche	Fr. Ponziglione	Annuity Rolls	F. La-Flesche
A			**C (cont.)**		
			che	kah	ho^n
a	ah	a	che	sha	çe
a	ah	tha	che	she	zhe
a	ap	a	chi	che	ts'i^n
an	han	none	chi	che	xe
an	hon	ho^n	chi	che	xthe
an	hun	ho^n	chi	he	xi^n
aus	o	o	chi	ke	xthe
aus	os	none	chi	keh	hi^n
			chi	she	zhi
C			chie	ka	xthe
			chie	kah	ga
c	se	c	chie	ke	gi
ca	ka	ka	chie	keh	ki^n
ch	k	none	chie	key	none
ch	sh	none	chre	hrah	xtha
cha	ka	xthe	chre	hre	xtha
cha	kah	ko^n	chre	hre	xthi
chai	sha	sha	chre	hre	xthi^n
chan	chon	xo^n	chta	sha ta	sha ta
chan	kan	none	chta	sha tah	sha ta
chan	kon	ko^n	ci	se	ç
chan	shon	zho^n	ck	se ka	çi ka
che	che	chi	cke	se kah	çi ka
che	che	xi	ckta	se ka tah	none
che	che	cthi	com	ko	l'o
che	he	xe	com	kon	ko^n
che	he	xi	con	ko	k'o
che	ka	xthe	con	kon	ko^n

D   G (cont.)

da	da	none	gre	gra	gthe
da	dah	none	gre	grah	gtha
da	ta	ta	gre	grah	gthe
da	tah	da	gre	grah	gtho^n
di se	te sa	ts'a	gre	grah	on be
di	te	ti	gre	gre	gthe
di	teh	ti	gri	gre	gthi
di	ti	ti			
dra	tah	da		**H**	

E

			ha	ha	hi^n
			ha	ha	xa
e	a	e	ha	hah	ha
e	e	i	ha	hah	we thi^n
e	i	e	ha	hah	xa
eh	a	e	ha	ho	ho^n
eh	e	i	ha	hop	a
eh	ea	none	han	an	wo^n
			han	han	none
	G		han	ho	ho·^{n}
			han	hon	ho^n
g	g	gi	han	hun	ho^n
g	k	none	ha pe	ap pe	a be
ga	gah	ga	ha pe	ap py	a be
ga	kah	ga	ha pe	hop pe	a be
ga chre	gah hre	gthi^n	ha pe	hop py	a be
ga he	gah heh	gthe	he	he	he
gi	ge	xthe	he	he	xe
gka	g	gi	hi	he	hi
gka	kah	ko^n	hin	he	hi^n
g ke	ka	xthe	hin	heh	xe
g'ke	kah	k'a	hin	hen	xi^n
g ki	ke	xthe	his	e	i
gku	koh	ko^n	his	e	i^n
gra	gla	gthe	his	en	i^n
gra	gra	gthe	hissa	e'sah	none
gra	grah	gtha	hu	ho	ho
gra	grah	gthe	hu	ho	ho^n
gra	grah	gtho^n	hu	hon	ho^n
gra	grah	on be	hu	hu	hi^n

hu	hu	hiu
hu	hu	hu
hu	hu	ki^n
hu	hun	ho^n
hum	hum	ho^n

I

i	e	i
ich	e'ka	none
ich	e'sh	none
in	en	i^n
in	in	i^n

K

k	ka	ga
ka	kah	ka
kru	gro	none
kru	gru	gthu

L

la	ka	xthe
la	kah	ga
la	la	the
la	lah	the
le	ka	k'a
le	kah	ka
le	ka	xthe
le	ke	ke
le	keh	ki^n
le	la	the
le	lah	the
le	le	thi
le	le	thi^n
lo	ko	k'o
lo	koh	ko^n
lo	lo	tho
lo	loh	tho

L (cont.)

lu	ko	k'o
lu	koh	ho^n
lu	lo	tho
lu	loh	tho

M

ma	ma	ma
ma	mah	ma
ma	mon	mo^n
man	mo	mo^n
man	moh	mo^n
me	me	mi
mi	me	mi
mi	me	wi^n
min	me	mi
min	men	wi^n
mint	me	mi
mint	meh	wi^n
mis	me	mi
mit	me	mi

N

na	na	no^n
na	nah	no^n
nam	nam	no^n
nam	nan	no^n
nam	nom	no^n
nam	non	hno^n
nam	nun	no^n
nas	na	no^n
nas	nah	no^n
ni	ne	ni
nin	ne	ni
num	nom	no^n
num	non	no^n
num	num	no'^{n}
num	nun	no^n

O			S (cont.)		
on	um	none	su	su	çu
			su	sy	none
			sue	we	wi

P

T

pa	pa	ba			
pa	pah	pa	ta	ta	ta
pe	pa	þa	ta	tah	da
pe	pah	ba	ta	to	to^n
pe	pe	be	ta	toh	to^n
pe	pe	xpe	tan	toh	ta
			tan	tom	ta
	S		tan	tom	to^n
			tan	ton	to^n
sa	sah	çe	tan	tun	to^n
sa	sop	ça	ta sa	tah sah	ts'a
san	son	ço^n	taw	tah	da
san	sun	none	taw	tow	to^n
sans	sah	çe	tce	tsa	dse
scha	scah	çka	tce	tse	dse
se	sa	çe	tchi	tish	tsi
se	sah	çe	tchi	tse	dse
se	she	zhi^n	tchi	tsi	tze
sha	sha	sha	tchi	tshe	none
sha	shah	sha	te	ta	da
shan	shon	zho^n	te	tah	da
she	she	zhi	tha	tah	ta
shi	she	zhi	toe	to e	none
shie	sea	çi a	ton	ton	to^n
shie	se'a	çi a	ton	tun	to^n
shin	shin	xthi	tsde	tse	dse
shu	sho	none	tse	tse	dse
shu	shon	zho^n	tse	tse	ts'i^n
shu	shop	zha	tsha	tsah	tse
shu	shu	zhiu	tshe	tsa	tse
shun	shon	zho^n	tsi	tse	dse
si	se	ç	tssi	tse	tsi
soi	wa	wa	tssi	tsi	tse
soi	wah	wa	tsy	tsy	dse
son	sah	çe	tu	to	to

T (cont.)

tza	tsa	tse
tze	tsa	tse
tze	tse	tsi
tze	tsy	dse
tzi	tse	tse
tzie	tsch	none

U

u	o	o
u	u	u
u	u	zhu
ui	ue	zhu
ui	we	wi
um	um	none
us	uz	none
us	y	none
us	ys	none

V

vi	we	wi

W

we	wa	wa
we	wah	wa
we	we	wi
we	weh	none
wha	wah	wa
whas	wah	wa
win	we	wi
wue	we	wi

Z

ze	sa	çi
ze	sa	sha
ze	sah	sha

166

OSAGE INDIAN
BIBLIOGRAPHY

This bibliography is given in two parts. The first part is annotated from references in our personal Osage collection. In the second part, the annotations have been omitted since the sources have not as yet been added to our Osage collection. Included in this bibliography are 250 sources of Osage information.

ANNOTATED BIBLIOGRAPHY

Abbot, Charles Greeley, ed., The Smithsonian Series, v. 1, "Preserving the Story of the Indians," Smithsonian Institution Series, Inc.: New York, 1944. 381 pp., indexed (see pp. 118-120).
This article reports on some of the activities of Dr. La Flesche. The tatooing ceremony is given in a sketch form.

Abel, Anna Heloise, "Indian Reservations in Kansas and the Extinguishment of their Title," Transactions of the Kansas State Historical Society, 1903-1904, v. 8, State Printer: Topeka, Kansas, 1904. 594 pp., indexed.
This paper has a fold out map of Indian reservations in Kansas. While the article deals with all Kansas tribes, it contains considerable Osage information. (Also see the index for other Osage information.)

Approved Roll of Osage Indians in Oklahoma, ca 1921. 77 pp., indexed.
This printed roll was approved in the summer of 1921. It has two indexes, one is for those less than half bood and the other for those of more than half blood.

Ashcraft, Allan C., "Confederate Indian Department Conditions, 1864," Chronicles of Oklahoma, v. 41, no. 3, Autumn, 1963:270-285.
Does not contain much Osage information. The article is worth reading because it gives a Southern view and treatment of Indian affairs.

Atherton, Lewis E., "Missouri's Society and Economy in 1821," Missouri Historical Review, v. 65, no. 4, July 1971:450-477.
The main thrust is American culture in Missouri. Indian references are scattered mention of the Osages. Excellent background for understanding the Osage Treaty of 1825.

Auger, Roland J., La Grand Recrue de 1653, Publication de la Societe Genealogique Canadienne Française, no. 1, Montreal, 1955.
We have a few photostats of this reference. The book gives biographical sketches of all the persons who came to Montreal in 1653.

Bailey, Garrick A., "The Osage Roll: An Analysis," Indian Historian, v. 5, no. 1, Spring, 1972: 26-29.
Mr. Bailey is either biased in his presentation or has ignored the available evidence. The Catholic Church records of St. Charles, Westport, and Osage Mission clearly refute most of his bold assertions. In the light of many obvious errors, one should proceed with caution in using this material.

Baird, W. David, "Fort Smith and the Red Man," Arkansas Historical Quarterly, v. 30, no. 4, Winter, 1971:337-348.
Limited and scattered Osage reference. Mainly concerned with immigrant tribes and Fort Smith in the Civil War.

_____, W. David, The Osage People, Indian Tribal Series: Phoenix, Arizona, 1972. 103 pp.
One of the best sketch histories of the Osages available. Very little new information since

it comes from secondary sources.

Bancroft, Hubert Howe, Bancrofts Works, vols. 27-28, or History of the Northwest Coast, vols. 1-2, 1543-1800 and 1800-1846, A. L. Bancroft and Company: San Francisco, 1884.

Several of the Osage-French were associated with the Lewis and Clark Expedition and the Astorians. These are discussed by Bancroft. Also several Osage-French families settled in what is now Tumwater, Washington in the 1840's.

Bartles, W. L., "Massacre of Confederates by Osage Indians in 1863," Transactions of the Kansas State Historical Society, 1903-1904, v. 8, State Printer: Topeka, Kansas, 1904. 594 pp. indexed (pp. 62-66).

There are several accounts of this event. This account has information not found in other accounts. (Also see the index for other Osage information.)

Bass, N.W., et al, Subsurface Geology and Oil and Gas Resources Osage County, Oklahoma, U.S. Dept. of the Interior Geological Survey Bulletin 900-A, Federal Prison Industries Inc.: El Reno, Oklahoma, 1952 (pp. 1-48).

Part 1, Townships 22 and 23 north, Ranges 10 and 11 east, Southeastern Osage County. Has large map tables. This is a well log study.

_____, N.W., et al, Subsurface Geology and Oil and Gas Resources Osage County, Oklahoma, U.S. Dept. of the Interior Geological Survey Bulletin 900-I, Federal Prison Industries, Inc.: El Reno,° Oklahoma, 1952 (pp. 330-349).

Part 9, Townships 23 and 24 north, Range 7 east, 6 miles west of Hominy, 9 miles southwest of Pawhuska. Has a large map and tables. This is a well log study.

_____, N.W., et al, Subsurface Geology and Oil and Gas Resources Osage County, Oklahoma, U.S. Dept. of the Interior Geological Survey Bulletin 900-J, Federal Prison Industries, Inc.: El Reno, Oklahoma, 1952 (pp. 350-374).

Part 10, Burbank and South Burbank oil fields, Townships 26 and 27 north, Range 5 east, and Townships 25 to 27 north, Range 6 east. Has a large map and tables. This is a well log study.

_____,N.W., Subsurface Geology and Oil and Gas Resources Osage County, Oklahoma, U.S. Dept. of the Interior Geological Survey Bulletin 900-K, Federal Prison Industries, Inc.: El Reno, Oklahoma, 1952 (pp. 375-428) index.

Part 11, summary of subsurface geology with special reference to oil and gas. Has a large map, tables and illustrations.

Bearss, Ed and Arrell M. Gibson, Fort Smith: Little Gibralter on the Arkansas, University of Oklahoma Press: Norman, 1969, 349 pp., indexed.

Contains significant information about the Claremore bands. Presents an unbiased account of the massacre at Claremore's Mound.

_____, Edwin C., "In Quest of Peace on the Indian Border: The Establishment of Fort Smith," Arkansas Historical Quarterly, v. 23, no. 2, Summer, 1964:123-153.

Primarily a Cherokee article. Mention of Osages is very scattered. Does not contain any significant Osage information.

Bell, Ovid, A History of Côte Sans Dessein, Ovid Bell Press: Fulton, Missouri, 1930. 94 pp., indexed.

For many Osage-French mixed bloods this is an invaluable source of information. It contains many eye witness accounts and shows deep research into primary sources.

Berry, Brewton, Carl Chapman, and John Mack, "Archaeological Remains of the Osage," American Antiquity, v. 10, no. 1, July 1944:1-11.

An excellent article. It describes and gives a map of the Osage sites in Missouri. The sites at the Osage, Little Osage, Marmaton Rivers junction are discussed.

Bloodworth, Jessie, et al, The Osage People and their Trust Property, A Field Report of the BIA Anadarko Area Office, Osage Agency, 1953.

Contains considerable statistical information. Other than a brief historical sketch, it deals with the mineral trust.

Brewster, S.W., "Reverend Father Paul M. Ponziglione," Transactions of the Kansas Historical Society, 1905-1906, v. 9, State Printing Office: Topeka, Kansas, 1906. 654 pp., indexed (pp. 19-32).

Beginning with volume 12 the name Transactions was changed to Collections. Primarily about Fr. Ponziglione, S.J. Some Osage mention is made. (Also, see the index for other Osage information.)

Burchardt, Bill, "Osage Oil," Chronicles of Oklahoma, v. 41, no. 3, Autumn, 1963:253-269.

An excellent summary of the wholesale murder of Osages for their headrights.

Burns, Louis F., The Fur Trading Ventures of Auguste Pierre Chouteau and Pierre "Cadet" Chouteau, Masters Thesis, Kansas State University, Emporia, 1950.

Limited Osage information. Section on Col. August P. Chouteau deals somewhat with the Osage fur trade.

_____, Louis F., Osage Annuity Rolls of 1878, First Roll, Ciga Press: Fallbrook, California, 1981. Unpaged, 97 pp., indexed by annuity number.

Gives name, age, sex, relationship to head of household, annuity number, and band of each Osage. Supplemental information for most mixed bloods. A mortality graph is included.

_____, Louis F., Osage Annuity Rolls of 1878, Second Roll, Ciga Press: Fallbrook, California, 1981. Unpaged, 105 pp., two indexes by annuity number.

Has a list of clans. Includes a general index and an index of translated names. Gives name, age, sex, relationship to the head of the household, annuity number and band of each Osage. Supplemental information for most mixed bloods. Includes a sound spelling key.

_____, Louis F., Osage Annuity Rolls of 1878, Third Roll, Ciga Press: Fallbrook, California, 1981. Unpaged, 103 pp., two indexes by annuity numbers.

Has an index of translated names and a general index. Contains a correlated, limited, dictionary of English and La Flesche phonics. Also a sound spelling key. Roll gives name, age, sex, relationship to head of household, annuity number and band of each Osage.

_____, Louis F., "Old Trails Across Northern Osage County," Chronicles of Oklahoma, v. 59, no. 4, Winter, 1981-1982:422-429.

Traces several Osage trails. Has a map.

_____, Louis F., Turn of the Wheel, AM Graphics: San Marcos, California, 1980. 400 pp., indexed.

Contains a sketch history of the Osages. Many of the mixed blood families are traced back to France. Contains Fr. Point's map of Westport, 1840.

Burrill, Robert M., "The Establishment of Ranching on the Osage Reservation," Geographical Review, v. 62, no. 4, October, 1972:524-543.

The title describes the content very well. Has three maps showing cattle trails across Osage County and lease ranches in the county. Very well done article.

Busby, Orel, "Buffalo Valley: An Osage Hunting Ground," Chronicles of Oklahoma, v. 40, no. 1, Spring, 1962:22-35.

Has limited but pertinent Osage information. It is worth the time to read for Osage information.

Bushnell, David I., Jr., Burials of the Algonquin Siouan and Caddoan Tribes West of the Mississippi, Smithsonian, Bureau of Ethnology Bulletin 83, Government Printing Office: Washington, 1927. 103 pp., indexed (see pp. 55-60).

Excellent Osage information. Illustrated.

_____, David I., Jr., Villages of the Algonquian, Siouan, and Caddoan Tribes West of the Mississippi, Smithsonian, Bureau of Ethnology Bulletin 77, Government Printing Office: Washington, 1922. 211 pp., indexed (see pp. 98-108).

Excellent Osage information. Describes lodges, some bands and locations. Illustrated.

Chapman, Berlin B., "Dissolution of the Osage Reservation, Part One," Chronicles of Oklahoma,

v. 20, no. 3, September, 1942.

Excellent discussion of land use practices preceding allotment in 1906. Contains significant Osage information. Unfortunately, we could not obtain a copy of Part Two.

_____, Berlin B., "Removal of the Osages from Kansas, Part One," Kansas Historical Quarterly, v. 7, no. 3, August, 1938: 287-305.

Part Two [conclusion], v. 7, no. 4, November, 1938:399-410.

This is primarily a presentation of the political problems of removal. It treats with the acquisition of the present reservation and the problems of removal.

Chapman, Carl H., "Digging up Missouri's Past," Missouri Historical Review, v. 61, no. 3, April, 1967:348-363.

While this is a general report of Missouri archaeology, it contains some mention of the Osage.

Chase, Charles Monroe, "An Editor Looks at Early-Day Kansas: The Letters of Charles Monroe Chase," ed. Lela Barnes, Kansas Historical Quarterly, v. 26, 1960:118-151 (138-139 and 142-143).

Limited but significant information.

Chouteau, Frederick, "Reminiscences of Frederick Chouteau," Transactions of the Kansas State Historical Society, 1903-1904, v. 8, State Printer: Topeka, Kansas, 1904. 594 pp., indexed (see pp. 423-434).

Almost entirely about the Kaw. Chouteau does give some significant information about Clement Lessert. The main value of the article is the similiarity between the Osage and Kaw. (Also, see the index for Osage information.)

Connelley, William E., ed., Collections of the Kansas State Historical Society, 1913-1914, v. 13, Kansas State Printing Plant: Topeka, 1915. 602 pp., indexed.

Limited Osage information. See the index.

_____, William E., ed., Collections of the Kansas State Historical Society, 1919-1922, v. 15, Kansas State Printing Plant: Topeka, 1923. 673 pp., indexed.

Some relevant but limited Osage information on page 183.

_____, William E., ed., "Indian Treaties and Councils Affecting Kansas," Collections of the Kansas State Historical Society, 1923-1925, v. 16, Kansas State Printing Plant: Topeka, 1925. 900 pp., indexed (see p. 746).

A chronology of Indian transactions affecting Kansas. Gives dates, summaries, and participants. (Also, see the index for other Osage information.)

_____, William E., "Notes on the Early Indian Occupancy of the Great Plains," Collections of the Kansas State Historical Society, 1915-1918, v. 14, Kansas State Printing Plant: Topeka, 1918. 897 pp., indexed (see pp. 438-470).

Has two fold out maps. One map shows Caddoan and Siouan occupancy before the Siouan migration. The other map shows the Dhegiha penetration into Caddoan area by 1700. Gives Dorsey's tribal circle and Osage clans. Excellent information. (Also, see the index for other Osage information.)

_____, William E., ed., "Official Kansas Roster, 1854-1925," Collections of the Kansas State Historical Society, 1923-1925, v. 16, Kansas State Printing Plant: Topeka, 1925. 900 pp., indexed (see pp. 722-745).

Although the title gives the span of years as 1854-1925, the Indian offices start with 1805. This lists, Agents, Sub-Agents, and government employees at the Agencies. (Also, see the index for other Osage information.)

Connor, William, "The Lord's Prayer in Osage," American Indian, v. 3, no. 12, September, 1929:p. unknown.

Rendered in English phonics. Accent marks and syllabication omitted. Includes brief sketch on government interpreters.

Cory, C.E., "The Osage Ceded Lands," Transactions of the Kansas State Historical Society, 1903-1904, v. 8, State Printer: Topeka, Kansas, 1904. 594 pp., indexed (see pp. 187-199).

An excellent paper on the Ceded Lands. Traces the events leading to cession, the cession, and in the wake of cession. (Also, see the index for other Osage information.)

Cutler, Jervis, A Topographical Description of the State of Ohio, Indiana Territory, and Louisiana, originally published by C. Williams: Boston, 1812. Reprint, Garland Publishing, Inc.: N.Y., 1975 (see pp. 110-120).

The information in this volume is significant because of the date of first publication. It has one of the earliest American analyses of the Osages.

Cutler, W.G., History of the State of Kansas, A.T. Andreas: Chicago, 1883.

This is a huge work. Sometimes published in two volumes. Gives county histories. Invaluable sketch map for each county. See Neosho, Labette, and Montgomery Counties.

De Rosier, Arthur H., Jr., "William Dunbar Explorer," Journal of Mississippi History, v. 25, no. 3, July, 1963:165-185.

Good for background only. See pp. 169 and 171.

Dickerson, Philip, History of the Osage Nation, [No publishing facts given, published ca 1906-07.] 139 pp.

A pseudo scholary work. Typesetting poorly proofed. While this does contain some hard to find Osage information, much of it is based on hearsay evidence. Proceed with caution.

Dillard, W.R., et al, Subsurface Geology and Oil and Gas Resources Osage County, Oklahoma, U.S. Dept. of the Interior Survey Bulletin 900G, Federal Prison Industries, Inc.: El Reno, Oklahoma, 1952. pp. 256-291.

Part 7, Townships 20 and 21 north, Ranges 11 and 12 east, southeast area adjacent to Tulsa. Has a large map and tables. This is a well log study.

Dorsey, George A., "The Osage Mourning-War Ceremony," American Anthropologist, New Series, v. 4, no. 3, July-September, 1902:404-411.

Discusses a mourning ceremony at Pawhuska, April 1902. Sketchy but good information.

Dorsey, J. Owen, "Cults of the Omaha, Ponka, Kansa, and Osage," Smithsonian, Bureau of Ethnology, 11th Annual Report, 1889-1890, Government Printing Office: Washington, (see pp. 371-415).

This article is not specifically about the Osages. However, it does have Osage material and merits consideration. Very good background.

Dorsey, J. Owen, On the Comparative Phonology of Four Siouan Languages, Smithsonian, Annual Reports of the Board of Regents, 1883:919-929.

Compares Dakota, Dhegiha, Chewere, Winnebago, Mandan, Hidatsa, and Tutelo. Several dialects of these languages are given. For example, Ponca-Omaha, Kaw, Osage, and Quapaw are given under the Dhegiha language.

_____, J. Owen, Osage Traditions, Smithsonian, Bureau of Ethnology, 6th Annual Report, 1884-1885, Government Printing Office: Washington, 1888 (see pp. 375-397).

This is Dorsey's complete Osage Traditions with chart as given by Red Corn. In both English and in Osage. See Mallory for short version.

_____, J. Owen, "The Social Organization of the Siouan Tribes," Journal of American Folk-Lore, v. 4, no. 12, January-March, 1891:331-342 (see pp. 334-336).

In this article Dorsey presents his reconstruction of the Osage tribe. This is the symbolic fourteen clan organization and does not include the twenty-four clan organization.

Draper Collection, "George Rogers Clark Papers," Illinois Historical Collections.

The Clark Papers have lists of inhabitants of Vincennes, Kaskaskia, and Cahokia. Many Osage-French families are on these lists.

Early Catholic Church Records, Kansas City, Missouri [Westport], 1833-1845.

These records are in the archives of the parish of the Immaculate Conception Church, St.

171

Mary's, Kansas. See the Kickapoo Mission Register, the Sugar Creek Mission Register and the Westport Church Register. Considerable Osage-French information.

Favour, Alpheus H., Old Bill Williams, Mountain Man, University of Oklahoma Press: Norman, 1981. 234 pp., indexed.

As a young man Bill Williams married into the Osage tribe. His biography has some Osage information.

Ferber, Edna, Cimarron, Grosset and Dunlap, Publishers: N.Y., 1930. 388 pp.

This novel has some direct reference to the Osage.

Finney, Frank F., "Old Osage Customs Die with the Last Pah-hue-skah," Chronicles of Oklahoma, v. 36, no. 2, Summer, 1958:131-136.

Relates incidents in the lives of the Pa hue scah line. Contains worthwhile Osage information.

_____, Frank F., "The Osages and Their Agency," Chronicles of Oklahoma, v. 36, no., Winter, 1958-1959:416-428.

Excellent information revolving around the Osage Agent Isaac T. Gibson. Well researched.

_____, Frank F., "The Osage Indians and the Liquor Problem before Statehood," Chronicles of Oklahoma, v. 34, no. 4, Winter, 1956-1957:456-464.

Traces the liquor problem from ca 1800 to allotment in 1906. Deals primarily with the effects.

_____, Frank F., "Progress in the Civilization of the Osage," Chronicles of Oklahoma, v. 40, no. 1, Spring, 1962:2-21.

An excellent article which discusses the political and social events leading up to allotment.

Fitzgerald, Sister Mary Paul, Beacon on the Plains, Saint Mary College: Leavenworth, Kansas, 1939. 297 pp., indexed.

An especially well done history of Osage Mission. Excellent extensive bibliography. Rich in Osage information. Although she does not mention it, the Fitzgeralds lived with the Osages in what was known as the Irish Settlement.

Fitzpatrick, W.S., Treaties and Laws of the Osage Nation, Cedar Vale Commercial: Cedar Vale, Kansas, 1895. Reprint, Louis F. Burns, Santa Ana, California, 1967. 103 pp. + 19, indexed.

Contains all Osage Treaties except the Confederate Treaty. Also has the Constitution of 1881 and the laws enacted under that Constitution, in effect in 1895.

Fletcher, Alice and Francis La Flesche, "Location; Linguistic Relationships," Smithsonian, Bureau of Ethnology, 27th Annual Report, 1905-1906, Government Printing Office: Washington, 1911 (see pp. 57-66).

This gives a history sketch and then enters into tribal kinship groups. An adoption ceremony is also given as well as legends by clans.

Foreman, Grant, Advancing the Frontier, University of Oklahoma Press: Norman, 1968. 363 pp., indexed.

Contains a large amount of Osage information. Well written and well researched.

_____, Grant, Indians and Pioneers, University of Oklahoma Press: Norman, 1967. 300 pp., indexed.

This contains a quantity of information about Claremore's bands. Also has a fold out map. Well researched.

Gabler, Mrs. Ina, "Lovely's Purchase and Lovely County," Arkansas Historical Quarterly, v. 19, no. 1, Spring, 1960:31-39.

In the main, this article treats with the Cherokee. Osages are included only as necessary to present the Cherokee view. Includes maps.

Garrison, Blanche O., Letters of Blanche Michels Garrison, 1966-1975.

These letters were written to Louis F. Burns. They constitute a large body of information about the Osage mixed bloods.

Gibson, A.M., "Indian Territory United Nations, 1845" Chronicles of Oklahoma, v. 39, no. 4, Winter, 1961-1962:398-413.
    Very little Osage information. However, Black Dog's speech merits examination.
Giles, Janice Holt, Johnny Osage, Houghton Mifflin Company: Boston, 1960. 288 pp.
    This is a novel cast against an accurate historical background. The setting is the "three forks" area among the Claremore bands.
Goodrich, H.B., et al, Subsurface Geology and Oil and Gas Resources Osage County, Oklahoma, U.S. Dept. of the Interior Geological Survey Bulletin 900F, Federal Prison Industries, Inc.: El Reno, Oklahoma, 1952. pp. 224-255.
    Part 6, Township 28 north, Ranges 10 and 11 east, northeastern Osage County, Pond Creek-Caney River area. Has a large map and tables. This is a well log study.
Goodrich, James W., "In the Earnest Pursuit of Wealth: David Waldo in Missouri and the Southwest, 1820-1878," Missouri Historical Review, v. 66, no. 2, January, 1972:155-184.
    Excellent background information. Mention of Osages is coincidental. Very little Osage information.
Graves, William W., The First Protestant Osage Missions, 1820-1837, The Carpenter Press: Oswego, Kansas, 1949. 272 pp., indexed.
    Primarily a well organized collection of missionary letters. Graves does a wonderful job of linking the letters into a running narrative and withholds editing of the letters. Considerable Osage information given by eye witnesses.
Gregg, Kate L., The Road to Santa Fe: The Journal and Diaries of George Champlin Sibley, University of New Mexico Press: Albuquerque, 1969. 280 pp., indexed.
    Although this work hardly mentions the Osage, Major Sibley was Osage Agent at this time. The footnotes and bibliography should be very helpful in Osage research.
Griffith, C.R., The Eventful Missouri River, Mss. ca 1950.
    Mr. Griffith was Chief Channel Inspector from St. Charles to Rulo, Nebraska, on the Missouri River. He relates several stories about the Osages along the Missouri.
Haines, Joe D., Jr., "John Stink: The Osage Who Returned from the Grave," Chronicles of Oklahoma, v. 60, no. 1, Spring, 1982:34-41.
    Very little new information about Ho to moie. However, for one who is not familiar with the Ho to moie stories it is well worth reading.
Hodge, Frederick Webb, ed., Handbook of American Indians North of Mexico, Smithsonian, Bureau of American Ethnology, Bulletin 30, Government Printing Office: Washington, 1910. (see pp. 156-159).
    This is an encyclopedia type article. We believe it is more accurate than most popular references about the American Indian tribes.
Houck, Louis, A History of Missouri from the Earliest Explorations and Settlements Until the Admission of the State Into the Union, 3 vols., Reprint Edition, Arno Press, Inc.: N.Y., 1971. v. 1, 404 pp.; v. 2, 418 pp.; v. 3, 380 pp.; indexed.
    A standard reference on Missouri Frontier History. Contains excellent Osage information. Osage-French will find these volumes invaluable.
Hunter, John D., Manners and Customs of Several Indian Tribes, originally published in 1823, Reprint, Ross and Haines, Inc.: Minneapolis, 1957. 402 pp.
    This autobiography is by an Osage captive. Aside from customs he describes a journey of an Osage hunting party into the Rocky Mountains. Of special interest is a long list of plants used as medicine by the Osages.
Hunt, John, The Grey Horse Legacy, Bantam Books: N.Y., 1970. 392 pp.
    This is presented as fiction. The veil is thin and comes close to revealing some events at Gray Horse. [The different spelling of Gray Horse should be noted.]
Ingenthron, Elmo, Indians of the Ozark Plateau, School of the Ozarks Press: Point Lookout, Missouri, 1981. 182 pp., index.

Excellent Osage information. A vast improvement over the usual popular, American Indian reference. Based on primary and secondary sources.

In the Matter of the Claim of Kingsbery and Holmsley for Relief, etc., Testimony given before the U.S. Indian Agent July 29, 1875 at Pawhuska, Oklahoma. 59 pp. + 2.
   Although this is directed toward the loss of cattle in the Osage, it contains Osage information. It gives many names and locations.

Irving, Washington, A Tour on the Prairies, edited by John Francis McDermott, University of Oklahoma Press: Norman, 1962. 216 pp.
   Irving touches on both the White Hair bands and Claremore's bands. He deals more in depth with Claremore's bands than he does with the White Hair bands.

Jump, Kenneth Jacob, Osage Indian Poems and Short Stories, privately printed, 1979. 76 pp.
   The late Kenneth Jump wrote these poems and stories from tribal memory. Contains valuable information.

Kennedy, L.E., et al, Subsurface Geology and Oil and Gas Resources Osage County, Oklahoma, U.S. Dept. of the Interior Geological Survey Bulletin 900D, Federal Prison Industries, Inc.: El Reno, Oklahoma, 1952. pp. 141-184.
   Part 4, Townships 24 and 25 north, Ranges 10 and 11 east, east-central area, southwest of Bartlesville. Has large map and tables. This is a well log study.

_____, L.E., et al, Subsurface Geology and Oil and Gas Resources Osage County, Oklahoma, U.S. Dept. of the Interior Geological Survey Bulletin 900E, Federal Prison Industries, Inc.: El Reno, Oklahoma, 1952. pp. 185-223.
   Part 5, Townships 26 and 27 north, Ranges 10 and 11 east, northeastern Osage County. Has a large map and tables. This is a well log study.

Kirk, C.T., et al, Subsurface Geology and Oil and Gas Resources Osage County, Oklahoma, U.S. Dept. of the Interior Geological Survey Bulletin 900B, Federal Prison Industries, Inc.: El Reno, Oklahoma, 1952. pp. 49-88.
   Part 2, Townships 22 and 23 north, Ranges 8 and 9 east, Hominy area. Has large map and tables. This is a well log study.

_____, C.T., et al, Subsurface Geology and Oil and Gas Resources Osage County, Oklahoma, U.S. Dept. of the Interior Geological Survey Bulletin 900H, Federal Prison Industries, Inc.: El Reno, Oklahoma, 1952. pp. 292-329.
   Part 8, parts of Township 20 north, Ranges 9 and 10 east, and Township 21 north, Ranges 8 and 9 east, and all of Township 21 north, Range 10 east, Osage City-Prue area. Has a large map and tables. This is a well log study.

Knudson, Jerry W., "Newspaper Reaction to the Louisiana Purchase," Missouri Historical Review, v. 63, no. 2, January, 1969:182-213.
   Although this has scant mention of the Osage, the background information is valuable.

La Flesche, Francis, A Dictionary of the Osage Language, Smithsonian, Bureau of Ethnology Bulletin 109, Reprint, Indian Tribal Series: Phoenix, Arizona, 1975. 406 pp. + 15.
   An elaborate reprint of La Flesche's Osage Dictionary. This is the only edition still in print. Contains Osage-English and English-Osage. The phonics are mixed German-French.

_____, Francis, "Ceremonies and Rituals of the Osage," Smithsonian, Miscellaneous Collections, v. 63, no. 8, 1914:66-69.
   This is a field report of work in progress. Some information is in the report but it is mainly concerned with the methods used to acquire information.

_____, Francis, "Ethnology of the Osage Indians," Smithsonian Miscellaneous Collections, v. 76, no. 10, 1924:104-107.
   A report of work in progress. Contains some valuable information. Illustrated.

_____, Francis, "Osage Marriage Customs," American Anthropologist, v. 14, 1912: 127-130.

An excellent discussion of Osage marriage customs. Touches on ceremonial, non-ceremonial, and co-habitation marriages.

_____, Francis, "Osage Songs and Rituals," Smithsonian, Miscellaneous Collections, v. 65, no. 6, 1915:78-81.

This is a field report and it does not present more than an overview of work in progress. It does contain some interesting information and insights.

_____, Francis, "Osage Tribal Rites, Oklahoma," Smithsonian, Miscellaneous Collections, v. 72, no. 1, 1920:71-73.

A field report of work in progress. Some interesting information, which is incidental, in the report.

_____, Francis, "The Osage Tribe: Rite of the Chiefs; Sayings of the Ancient Men," Smithsonian, Bureau of Ethnology, 36th Annual Report, 1914-1915, Government Printing Office: Washington, 1921. 604 pp., indexed.

The paper is given in both English and Osage. An excellent history of the Osage is given as well as a listing of the clans. This is a rich source of Osage information.

_____, Francis, "The Osage Tribe: Rite of the Wa-Xo-Be," Smithsonian, Bureau of Ethnology, 45th Annual Report, 1927-1928, U.S. Printing Office: Washington, 1930. 857 pp., indexed (see pp. 523-857).

Rendered in both English and Osage. This work not only gives the full ceremonies of the Wa ho pe, but it also gives considerable background. A large amount of clan information is included.

_____, Francis, "The Osage Tribe: The Rite of Vigil," Smithsonian, Bureau of Ethnology, 39th Annual Report, 1917-1918, Government Printing Office: Washington, 1925. 636 pp.

This large work is given in both English and Osage. It encompasses many rituals of every day Osage life. It is one of the few sources for these rituals available today.

_____, Francis, "The Osage Tribe: Two Versions of the Child-Naming Rite," Smithsonian, Bureau of Ethnology, 43rd Annual Report, 1925-1926, U.S. Government Printing Office: Washington, 1928 (see pp. 23-164).

Given in both English and Osage versions. It has many of the clans and about forty pages of clan names for men and women. Invaluable for Osage family research.

_____, Francis, "Researches Among the Osages," Smithsonian, Miscellaneous Collections, v. 70, no. 2, 1919:110-113.

This field report contains excellent Osage information. Illustrated.

_____, Francis, "The Symbolic Man of the Osage Tribe," Art and Archaeology, v. 9, January-July, 1920:68-72.

In this article, La Flesche sets forth his reconstruction of the origins of the Osage religion. He also includes the origins of the gentile organization of the tribe. Of course, the religion and gentile organization overlap.

_____, Francis, "Tribal Rites of Osage Indians," Smithsonian, Miscellaneous Collections, v. 68, no. 12, 1918:84-90.

A field report about collecting information about Osage tribal rites. Scattered throughout the report are some "gems" of Osage information.

_____, Francis, "War Ceremony and Peace Ceremony of the Osage Indians," Smithsonian, Bureau of Ethnology Bulletin 101, U.S. Government Printing Office: Washington, 1939. 280 pp., indexed.

Excellent source of Osage information. Given in both English and Osage.

_____, Francis, "Work Among the Osage Indians," Smithsonian, Miscellaneous Collections, v. 66, no. 17, 1917:118-121.

Like most of the material in the Miscellaneous Collections, this is a field report of work in progress. The primary value is to give insights into the later full reports.

Lamb, Arthur H., The Osage People, Osage Printery: Pawhuska, Oklahoma, ca 1940.
Mostly repeats from Tragedies of the Osage Hills. Some new material.

Lamb, Arthur H., Tragedies of the Osage Hills, Osage Printery: Pawhuska, Oklahoma, ca 1924. 203 pp.
Many Osage stories, some are eyewitness accounts others are newspaper accounts. Majority of tales relate to the Osage Hills.

Mac Ritchie, David, "A Red Indian Coiffure," Man, v. 17, no. 1-138, 1917:7-9.
Largely a description of the Osage roach. Quoted almost entirely from Ruxton's Journal.

Mallory, Garrick, "Coloration of Pictographs," Smithsonian, Bureau of Ethnology, 10th Annual Report, 1888-1889, Government Printing Office, 1893 (see pp. 221-633).
This refers to obtaining colors and tattooing by the Osages. Specific Osage allusions are scattered.

_____, Garrick, "Pictographs of the North American Indians-Traditions," Smithsonian, Bureau of Ethnology, 4th Annual Report, 1882-1883, U.S. Printing Office: Washington, 1886 (see pp. 84-86).
This paper gives J. Owen Dorsey's Osage tradition of origin as related by Red Corn, but in an abridged form.

Martin, George W., ed., Collections of the Kansas State Historical Society, 1909-1910, v. 11, State Printing Office: Topeka, Kansas, 1910. 742 pp., indexed.
Excellent Osage information, but scattered. See the index. This information relates to little known events in Osage activities.

_____, George W., ed., Transactions of the Kansas State Historical Society, 1907-1908, v. 10, State Printing Office: Topeka, Kansas, 1908. 767 pp., indexed.
This volume contains many scattered bits of Osage information. Although it would take some labor to extract the information, the reward would be great.

Mathews, John Joseph, The Osages: Children of the Middle Waters, University of Oklahoma Press: Norman, 1961. 826 pp., indexed.
This is the best ethno-history of the Osages available. It does not use a typical history format or style.

_____, John Joseph, Sundown, Longman, Green and Co.: New York, 1934. 312 pp.
A mixed fiction of composite characters. It traces the conflicts within an Osage as he tries to assimilate into the American culture.

_____, John Joseph, Talking to the Moon, University of Chicago Press: Chicago, 1945. 244 pp.
In our opinion, this is the best work of Mathews. It traces a year of activities by the Osage calendar. A clear picture of the people living in the Osage Hills during the 1930's is given.

_____, John Joseph, Wah' Kon-Tah, University of Oklahoma Press: Norman, 1932. 359 pp.
A biography of Major Laban Miles, Osage Superintendent. It is also an account of the Osages stepping from barbarism into the American Civilization.

McDermott, John Francis, "The Indian as Human Being," Nebraska History, v. 52, no. 1, Spring, 1971:45-49.
McDermott seeks to place the Indian in his circumstance rather than the fiction of noble or mean circumstance. Special reference to Irving and Tixier among the Osage.

_____, John Francis, ed., Tixier's Travels on the Osage Prairies, University of Oklahoma Press: Norman, 1968. 309 pp., indexed.
Tixier describes his stay with the Osages at the Osage villages in Missouri. Contains information about bands, clans, and Osage families.

McGee, W.J., "The Siouan Indians: A Preliminary Sketch," Smithsonian, Bureau of Ethnology, 15th Annual Report, 1893-1894, Government Printing Office: Washington, 1897 (see pp. 157-195, 205-238).

This contains excellent background information. It was written to honor and introduce J. Owen Dorsey's posthumous, Siouan Sociology. Dorsey's article follows McGee's introduction.

Mitchell, Michael Dan, "Acculturation Problems Among the Plains Indians," Chronicles of Oklahoma, v. 44, no. 3, Autumn, 1966:281-289.
Contains some worthwhile Osage information.

Montagu, M.F. Ashley, "An Indian Tradition Relating to the Mastodon," American Anthropologist, New Series, v. 46, no. 4, 1944:568-571.
This article relates an Osage legend of large animals. It is background for the Osage terms of Big Bone and Little Bone Osages. These terms may, in part, be responsible for the Big Osage and Little Osage terms.

Moore, Raymond C., et al, The Kansas Rock Column, University of Kansas: Lawrence, 1951. 131 pp., indexed.
Since early Osage oil production was next to the Kansas-Oklahoma line, it is well to be aware of the strata names used in both states.

Morgan, Lewis H., The Indian Journals, 1859-1862, University of Michigan: Ann Arbor, 1959 (see p. 82, also preface).
Contains some brief but worthwhile comments about the Osages.

_____, Lewis H., Systems of Consanguinity and Affinity of the Human Family, Smithsonian, Contributions to Knowledge, v. 17, 1871, Smithsonian Institution: Washington.
The Osage portion of this massive work is on pp. 292-382. This gives 167 kinship terms and compares the Osage terms to other Siouan groups.

Morrison, T.F., "The Osage Treaty of 1865," Collections of the Kansas State Historical Society, 1926-1928, v. 15, Kansas State Printing Plant: Topeka, 1928. 976 pp., indexed (see pp. 692-708).
An outstanding paper with hard to find Osage information. Excellent account of Alfred Bernard Canville and his Kansas post. Copy of the Canville Treaty of 1865. Also, see the index for other Osage information.

Morris, Wayne, "A.P. Chouteau, Merchant Prince," Chronicles of Oklahoma, v. 48, no. 2, Summer, 1970:155-163.
Contains good information relating to the Claremore bands. Primarily about the "three forks" and "saline" posts.

_____, Wayne, "Traders and Factories on the Arkansas Frontier," Arkansas Historical Quarterly, v. 28, no. 1, Spring, 1969:28-48.
This article contains considerable information about the Claremore bands. It also has some excellent background information.

Nett, Betty R., "Historical Changes in the Osage Kinship System," Southwestern Journal of Anthropology, v. 8, 1952:164-181.
The textual comparison between Morgan's kinship terms and terms collected in 1950 is excellent. However, the text and accompanying charts do not agree. If one ignores the charts, the article is excellent.

Newman, Tillie Karnes, The Black Dog Trail, The Christopher Publishing House: Boston, 1957. 221 pp., indexed.
An excellent history of the Black Dog band. Well worth studying.

Nuttall, Thomas, A Journal of Travels into the Arkansas Territory During the Year 1819, Savoie Lottinville, ed., University of Oklahoma Press: Norman, 1980. 361 pp., indexed.
While Osage information is limited, this journal does throw some light on the Claremore bands.

O-Jan-Jan-Win, "And 'Twas the Night before Christmas' with Osages," American Indian, v. 4, no. 3, December, 1929: not paged.

An account of a Christmas celebration hosted by the Osages. Various tribes were guests.

Olcott, Deana C., The Enchanted Hills, Osage Printery: Pawhuska, Oklahoma, 1948. 47 pp.

Contains a variety of Osage information. While most of this information is not new, the booklet does have some new firsthand information.

Osage Indians, 1907-1957, Semi-Centennial Celebration, Osage Agency: Pawhuska, Oklahoma, 1957. Unpaged, 65 pp.

Contains some excellent maps and many rare pictures. Also has a variety of Osage information.

Osage Indian Tribe, 1872-1972, Centennial Celebration, Osage Agency: Pawhuska, Oklahoma, 1972. Unpaged, 81 pp.

Contains many valuable photographs and biographies.

Osage Indian Troubles in Kansas, The. [No publication date or source given.]

A 68 page monograph about the murder of Osage hunters in Kansas. The murderers were sworn into the Kansas Militia with back-dated papers to protect them from punishment. A copy is in the University of Oklahoma, Norman, Frontier Collection.

Osage Mission Records of Baptism, Marriage, and Burials, 1820-1871.

Original is now at Kansas State Historical Society, Topeka. First half is mainly Irish and German settlers, with scattered mixed-blood entries. Second half has almost entirely Osage entries. Early entries in Latin and French. Microfilm available. Louis F. Burns is currently typing these entries and indexing them.

Parker, Doris Whitetail, Footprints on the Osage Reservation, Private Printing, 1982. 156 pp. + xviii, indexed.

Contains extracts of vital statistics from early newspapers. These relate to the Osage County area in Oklahoma, 1875-1907.

Petition for Compensation for Lands Ceded by the Treaty of November 10, 1808, Before the Indian Claims Commission. [No date given, filed under the Act of August 13, 1946, PL 726, 79th Congress.]

Includes a copy of the Treaty of 1808. Lists reasons for the claim.

Petition for Compensation for Lands Ceded by the Treaty of September 25, 1818, Before the Indian Claims Commission. [No date given, filed under the Act of August 13, 1946, PL 726, 79th Congress.]

Has a copy of the Treaty of 1818. Lists grounds for the claim.

Petition for Compensation for Lands Ceded by the Treaty of June 2, 1825, Before the Indian Claims Commission. [No date given, filed under the Act of August 13, 1946, PL 726, 79th Congress.]

Has a copy of the Treaty of 1825. Gives reasons for the claim. This treaty should not be confused with the Council Grove or Santa Fe Trail Treaty also made in 1825.

Petition to Committee on Territories of the House of Representatives, January 25, 1888.

This petition asks that Indian Reservations not be included in the proposed State of Oklahoma.

Phillips, Isaac, et al, Brand Register of the Elgin, Kansas Shipping Pens, 1887-1907.

Copies of this register have been deposited with both the Kansas and Oklahoma Historical Societies, with comments by Louis F. Burns. In Osage research, it is valuable only for the names and brands of Osage ranchers.

Pollock, William J., Agent, Laws of the Osage Nation Passed at Pawhuska, Osage Nation, in the Years 1883, 1884, and 1885, Indian Journal Steam Job Office: Muskogee, I.T., 1885, 12 pp.

These laws are well worth reading. In later publications, many of these laws were omitted because they had been repealed by the time later publications of Osage law were compiled.

Prucha, Francis Paul, ed., Documents of United States Indian Policy, University of Nebraska Press: Lincoln, 1975. 278 pp., indexed.

A general reference, but it has some direct Osage mention. Fills many gaps in Osage research.

Regulations to Govern the Leasing of Lands in the Osage Reservation, Oklahoma, For Oil and Gas Mining Purposes, Approved July 12, 1932. 32 pp.

A detailed description of oil and gas leasing regulations. Includes a sample form.

Rohrer, John H., "The Test Intelligence of Osage Indians," Journal of Social Psychology, v. 16, 1942:99-105.

According to test scores the Osage group is socially, educationally, and economically on a par with the average white population of the United States.

Sanders, J.G., Who's Who Among Oklahoma Indians, Trave Company: Oklahoma City, 1928.

A general Indian work. Over half of the entries are Osage. Most entries have photograph of subject person. All entries have biographies.

Shoemaker, Floyd Calvin, Missouri and Missourians, v. 1 of 5 vols., The Lewis Publishing Company: Chicago, 1943. v. 1, 1023 pp., indexed.

Scattered and random references to the Osages. No references to Osage-French mixed bloods. See the index.

Shoup, Earl Leon, "Indian Missions in Kansas," Collections of the Kansas State Historical Society, 1911-1912, v. 12, State Printing Office: Topeka, Kansas, 1912. 569 pp., indexed (see pp. 65-69).

This paper touches on the various missions among the Osages. Also, see the index for other Osage information. This is the first volume to be called Collections, all earlier volumes were called Transactions.

Sibley, George Champlin, "Extracts from the Diary of Major Sibley," Chronicles of Oklahoma, v. 5, no. 2, June, 1927:196-220.

Primary source information about the Osages. This describes a tour made by Major Sibley, Osage Agent, in the summer of 1811.

Smith, Betty White, ed., Osage County Profiles, Osage County Historical Society, ca 1978. 568 pp., unindexed, later index available.

This work has many biographies of Osages. An excellent source of information. Mrs. Ruth Blake Burns has made an index for this volume. Index 107 pp.

Snyder, J.F., "Were the Osages Mound Builders?" Smithsonian, Annual Reports of the Board of Regents, 1888:587-596.

Snyder dates from the period when Americans could not believe Indians could have built the mounds. Later theories conceive that survivors of the mound builders merged with the Dhegiha. However, the paper does contain some excellent Osage information.

Spaulding, George F., On the Western Tour with Washington Irving: The Journal and Letters of Count de Pourtales, University of Oklahoma Press: Norman, 1968. 96 pp., indexed.

Some mention of the White Hair bands. More information about the Claremore bands.

Subsurface Geology and Oil and Gas Resources Osage County, Oklahoma, U.S. Dept. of the Interior Geological Survey Bulletin 900-C, Federal Prison Industries, Inc.: El Reno, Oklahoma, 1952, pp. 89-140.

This bulletin is out of print and it is no longer available. It covers the Pawhuska, Oklahoma area. A new seismographic mapping of Osage County is currently being made using the osmosis process. Possibly this will be available in a few years. This current study should be far superior to the log studies of the 1950's.

Tanguay, L'Abbe Cyprien, Monseigneur Irenee Lussier, ed., Dictionnaire National des Canadiens Francais: 1608-1760, Institut Genealogique Drouin: Montreal, Canada, 1871.

For Osage-French mixed blood research these ponderous volumes are a must. Most of the early Osage-French families are included. Very little knowledge of French is required to follow this excellent work.

179

Tedlock, Barbara, "From Ceremony of Sending: A Simultanity for Twenty Choruses," Alcheringa, v. 1, no. 1, Autumn, 1970:52-56.

Alcheringa is a magazine of Indian tribal poetry. The Osage poem is taken from The Rite of the Chiefs. Four of the twenty-four clans did not participate in the vocal part of this ceremony, hence the chorus of only twenty.

_____, Barbara, "Planting Song," Alcheringa, v. 2, no. 2, Summer, 1971:35.

Alcheringa is a magazine of ethnopoetics. The Osage poem is a poetic presentation of the planting rite recorded by Alice Fletcher of the Smithsonian.

Tinker, George Edward and C.J. Phillips, eds., Osage Magazine. [Started publication ca 1909 at Pawhuska, Oklahoma and consolidated with the Oklahoma Stockman.]

No complete file of these magazines are known to exist. The few copies in our collection have a variety of Osage articles. These magazines are invaluable whenever copies can be found.

Tinker, Sylvester J., Authentic Osage Indian Roll Book, Sam McClain: Pawhuska, Oklahoma, 1957. 53 pp., indexed.

This is the final roll of 1906. Degree of Osage blood is given in this version, but this feature was not included in the original roll of 1906.

Tracey, Valerie, "The Indian in Transition: The Neosho Agency 1850-1861," Chronicles of Oklahoma, v. 48, no. 2, Summer, 1970:164-183.

Excellent article, well researched. Gives good Osage information, especially about mixed bloods. Fine sketch on Andrew J. Dorn, Osage Agent.

Underhill, Lonnie E. and John N. Battle, "Classification of Indian Tribes," Chronicles of Oklahoma, v. 48, no. 2, Summer, 1970:197-208.

Very little Osage information. A chart of language classifications by tribes offers some interesting information.

Wells, Frank Evarts, The Story of "Old Bill" Williams: Scout of the Santa Fe Trail, 4th edition, Williams News Press: Williams, Arizona. 14 pp.

A brief biography of Bill Williams. This pamphlet contains some Osage information.

Wedel, Waldo R., An Introduction to Kansas Archeology, Smithsonian, Bureau of American Ethnology, Bulletin 174, U.S. Government Printing Office: Washington, 1959 (see pp. 54-58).

This is an encyclopedia type account of the Osages. It is a very creditable piece of work.

Wheat, Joe Ben, "A Paleo-Indian Bison Kill," Scientific American, v. 216, no. 1, January, 1967: 44-52.

This is not an Osage article. It does give some insight into a hunting method and methods of butchering bison.

White, Lonnie J., "Arkansas Territorial Indian Affairs," Arkansas Historical Quarterly, v. 21, no. 3, Autumn, 1962: 193-212.

Some excellent background information. Limited, direct, Osage data. Mentions many Arkansas tribes, but primarily the immigrant tribes such as the Cherokee.

_____, Lonnie J., "The Election of 1827 and the Conway-Crittenden Duel," Arkansas Historical Quarterly, v. 19, no. 4, Winter, 1960: 293-313.

Only coincidental mention of the Osage. Little information of value to Osage research. Appears on some bibliographies of Osage materials. We mention it here to warn a researcher of its small value.

Wolff, Hans, "An Osage Graphemic Experiment," International Journal of American Linguistics, v. 24, no. 1, January, 1958: 30-35.

A follow-up study of two earlier studies into the characteristics of the Osage language.

_____, Hans, "Osage I: Phonemes and Historical Phonology," International Journal of American Linguistics, v. 18, no. 2, January, 1952: 63-68.

180

A study in the characteristics of Osage sounds and speech patterns.

———————, Hans, "Osage II: Morphology," International Journal of American Linguistics, v. 18, no. 4, October, 1952: 231-237.

A continuing study into the characteristics of the Osage language.

Zoltvany, Yves F., "New France and the West, 1701-1713," The Canadian Historical Review, v. 46, no. 4, December, 1965: 301-322.

Excellent background for the French fur trade movements. One casual, but important mention of the Osage on p. 318.

UNANNOTATED BIBLIOGRAPHY

Anderson, Harry H., Sioux Occupation of Missouri Territory, 1640-1868, Clearwater Publishing Co.: New York.

Atkeson, W.O., History of Bates County, Missouri, Topeka, Kansas, 1918.

Bailey, Garrick A., Changes in Osage Social Organization: 1673-1969, Dissertation Abstracts International, 31 (1970-1971):3812B. UM 71-1292.

Baird, Donald, "Some Eighteenth Century Gun Barrels from Osage Village Sites," Great Plains Journal, 4 (1964-1965):49-62.

Baptismal Register of St. Ferdinand's Church, The, 1792-1857, Archives of St. Ferdinand's Church, Florissant, Missouri.

Barney, R.A., Laws Relating to the Osage Tribe of Indians, Pawhuska, Oklahoma, 1929. 112 pp.

Chapman, Carl H. and Eleanor F. Chapman, Indians and Archaeology of Missouri, University of Missouri Press: Columbia, 1964. 161 pp., illus., maps [Missouri Handbook, 6].

_____, Carl H., "Continued Excavations on the Little Osage Indian Village Site in the Kaysinger Bluff Reservoir Area," Plains Anthropologist, 10 (1965):51.

_____, Carl H., Culture Sequence in the Lower Missouri Valley, in J.B. Griffin, ed., Archeology of Eastern United States, Chicago, 1952. 139-151.

_____, Carl H., The Origin of the Osage Indian Tribe: An Ethnographical, Historical Archaeological Study, Dissertation Abstracts, 20 (1959-1960):1525. UM 59-4894.

_____, Carl H., Osage Indians: The Origin of the Osage Indian Tribe: an Ethnographical Historical and Archaeological Study, Vol. 3 (American Indian Ethnohistory Ser: Plains Indians). Garland Publishers, Inc.: New York.

_____, Carl H., Osage Indian Village Sites and Hunting Territory in Kansas, Missouri, and Oklahoma, Clearwater Publishing Co.: New York.

_____, Carl H., "Osage Prehistory," Plains Anthropologist, 7 (1962):99-100.

Case, Nelson, History of Labette County, Kansas, Topeka, Kansas, 1893.

Christianson, James R., A Study of Osage History Prior to 1876, Dissertation Abstracts International, 30 (1969-1970):639A. UM 69-11, 202.

Corbitt, D.C., translator and ed., "Papers from the Spanish Archives Relating to Tennessee and the Old Southwest," East Tennessee Historical Society Publications, 31 (1959):63-82; 32 (1960):72-93; 33 (1961):61-78; 34 (1962):86-105; 35 (1963):85-95; 36 (1964):70-80; 37 (1965):89-105; 38 (1966):70-82; 39 (1967):87-102; 40 (1968):101-118; 41 (1969):100-116; 42 (1970):96-107; 43 (1971):94-111; 44 (1972):104-113.

Defouri, Fr. James, Osage Mission, Mss., Papers of Monsignor J.J. Shorter, Leavenworth Diocesan Chancery Office, Kansas City, Kansas.

Dodge, Henry, Journal of Colonel Dodge's Expedition from Fort Gibson to the Pawnee Pict Village, American State Papers, Military Affairs, 5 (1860):373-382.

Donaldson, T., The George Catlin Indian Gallery, United States National Museum, Reports (1885):42-46.

Dorsey, George A., "Traditions of the Osage," Field Museum, Anthropological Series, 7 (1904): 9-60.

Dorsey, James Owen, "An Account of the War Customs of the Osages," American Naturalist, 18 (1884):113-133.

Douglas, Fredric H., "An Osage Yarn Bag," Denver Art Museum, Material Culture Notes, 7 (1938):26-30.

Drinnon, Richard, White Savage: The Case of John Dunn Hunter, Schocken Books: New York, 1972. 282 pp.

Duncan, L. Wallace, ed., History of Montgomery County, Kansas, Iola Register: Iola, Kansas, 1903.

_ _ _ _, L. Wallace, ed., History of Neosho and Wilson Counties, Kansas, Fort Scott, Kansas, 1902.

Fay, George E., ed., Charters, Constitutions and By-Laws of the Indian Tribes of North America, Part 5: The Indian Tribes of Oklahoma, University of Northern Colorado: Greeley, Museum of Anthropology, Occasional Publications in Anthropology, Ethnology Series, 6, 1968. ERICED 046555.

Finney, Frank F., "Marie Tallchief, in History: Oklahoma's own Ballerina," Chronicles of Oklahoma, 38 (1960):8-11.

Finney, T.M., "Wahshwahgaley," Pioneer Days with the Osage Indians West of '96, Bartlesville, Oklahoma, 1925.

Garraghan, Gilber J., S.J., The Jesuits of the Middle United States, America Press: New York, 1938.

Graves, Mrs. W.W., "In the Land of the Osages: Harmony Mission," Missouri Historical Review, 19 (1925):409-418.

Graves, W.W., Annals of Osage Mission, St. Paul, Kansas, 1935.

_ _ _ _, W.W., Life and Letters of Rev. Fr. John Schoenmaker, S.J., Apostle to the Osages, The Commercial Publisher: Parsons, Kansas, 1928.

_ _ _ _, W.W., Life and Letters of Father Ponziglione, Schoenmakers and Other Early Jesuits at Osage Mission, St. Paul, Kansas, 1916.

Gregg, Kate L., "The History of Fort Osage," Missouri Historical Review, July, 1940.

_ _ _, Kate L., Westward with Dragoons, Fulton, Missouri, 1937. 97 pp.

Hargrett, L., A Bibliography of the Constitutions and Laws of the American Indians, 99-100, Cambridge, 1947.

Harner, J., "The Village of the Big Osage," Missouri Archaeologist, 5 (1939):19-20.

Henning, Dale R., The Osage Nation in Eastern Oklahoma and Northwest Arkansas, 1775-1818, Clearwater Publishing Co.: New York.

History of Jackson County, Missouri, Union Historical Society, Birdsell, Williams & Co.: Kansas City, Missouri, 1881.

History of Vernon County, Missouri, Brown and Co.: St. Louis, 1887.

Holway, Hope, "Union Mission, 1826-1837," Chronicles of Oklahoma, 40 (1962):355-378.

Howard, James H., The Osage Tribe: Divisions and Locations, History, and Numbers, Kansas City Museum Leaflets, 1, Kansas City Museum: Kansas City, Missouri, 1956.

Hoyt, George H., Kansas and the Osage Swindle, Washington, 1868. Pamphlet.

Indian Claims Commission, Osage Indians: Findings, Facts, and Opinion, Vol. 5 (American Indian Ethnohistory Ser: Plains Indians). Garland Publishing, Inc.: New York.

Jackson, Donald, "A New Lewis and Clark Map," Missouri Historical Society Bulletin, 17 (1960-1961):117-132.

La Barre, Weston, A Cultist Drug Addiction in an Indian Alcoholic, Menninger Clinic, Bulletin, 5 (1941):40-46.

_ _ _, Weston, The Peyote Cult, Yale University, Department of Anthropology: New Haven, Connecticut, 1938. 188 pp.

La Flesche, Francis, "Omaha and Osage Traditions of Separation," International Congress of Americanists, Proceedings, 19 (1915):459-462.

Lesser, Alexander, Siouan Kinship, Dissertation Abstracts, 19 (1958-1959):208. UM 58-2596.

Marriott, Alice, Osage Indians: Osage Research Report, and Bibliography of Basic Research References, Vol. 2 (American Indian Ethnohistory Ser.: Plains Indians), Garland Publishing, Inc.: New York.

Martin, Viahnett S., Years with the Osage, Edgemoor Publishing Co.: Houston, Texas, 1975.

McGimsey, Charles R., III, Indians of Arkansas, Arkansas Archeological Survey, Publications on Archeology, Popular Series, 1, Archeological Survey: Fayetteville, Arkansas, 1969. 7, 1-47.

McRill, Leslie A., "Ferdinandia: First White Settlement in Oklahoma," Chronicles of Oklahoma, 41 (1963):126-159.

Morfi, J.A. de, Memorias for the History of the Province of Texas, ed. by F.M. Chabot, San Antonio, Texas, 1932. 85 pp.

Morrison, T.F., "Mission Neosho: The First Kansas Mission," Kansas Historical Quarterly, 4, August, 1935:227-234.

Morse, Jedidiah, Report to the Secretary of War of the United States on Indian Affairs, New Haven, 1822.

Nasatir, Abraham F., "Ducharme's Invasion of Missouri, an Incident in the Anglo-Spanish Rivalry for the Indian Trade of Upper Louisiana," Missouri Historical Review, 24 (1929):3-25.

_____, Abraham F., Before Lewis and Clark, St. Louis, 1952. 2 vols., 882 pp.

Osage Indians, Vol. 4 (American Indian Ethnohistory Ser.: Plains Indians), Garland Publishing, Inc.: New York.

Parsons, David, Removal of the Osages from Kansas, A Doctoral Dissertation, University of Oklahoma, Norman.

Ponziglione, Paul M., S.J., "An Adventure of Lucille St. Pierre among the Osage," St. Louis Catholic Historical Review, 4 (1922):51-64.

_____ , Paul M., S.J., "Osage Indian Manners and Customs," St. Louis Catholic Historical Review, 4 (1922):130.

_____ _ ___ ___, Paul M., S.J., "Osage Mission during the Civil War," St. Louis Catholic Historical Review, 4 (1922):219-229.

Roger, T.F., History of Neosho County, Kansas, Monitor Printing Co.: Ft. Scott, Kansas, 1902.

Revard, Francis, Bartlesville [Oklahoma] Examiner, Articles about Osage history and life, Sunday issues, summer of 1935.

Riggs, S.R., "Dakota Grammar, Texts and Ethnography," Contributions to North American Ethnology, 9 (1893):18-29.

Rothensteiner, Rev. John, History of the Archdiocese of St. Louis, 2 vols. [see vol. I], Blackwell Wielandy Co.: St. Louis, 1928.

Sampson, Francis A., "Glimpses of Old Missouri by Explorers and Travelers," Missouri Historical Review, 1 (1907):247-266.

Scharf, J. Thomas, History of St. Louis, Louis H. Everts & Co.: Philadelphia, 1883.

School Register of St. Ann's Academy, 1886-1895, Archives of the Sisters of Loretto, Nerinx, Kentucky.

Shoemaker, Floyd C., "Osceola, Land of Osage River Lore," Missouri Historical Review, 54 (1959-1960):327-334.

Sibley, George C., "George C. Sibley's Journal of a Trip to the Salines in 1811," ed. by George R. Brooks, Missouri Historical Society, Bulletin, 21 (1954-1965):167-207.

__ _ _ . . ., George C., "Indian Mode of Life in Missouri and Kansas," Missouri Historical Review, October, 1914.

Skinner, Alanson B., "An Osage War Party," Public Museum of the City of Milwaukee, Year-book, 2 (1923):165-169.

Speck, Frank G., "Notes on the Ethnology of the Osage Indians," Pennsylvania University, Free Museum of Science and Art, Transactions, 2 (1907):159-171.

U.S. Congress, 25th Congress, 2d Session, Senate Document no. 59, Report of C.A. Harris, 27 December 1837; Report of Isaac McCoy, 26 October 1837 [Serial 314].

U.S. Congress, 25th Congress, 2d Session, Senate Document no. 467, Osage Relinquishment of School Lands, 7 March 1838 [Serial 318].

U.S. Congress, 30th Congress, 2d Session, House Document no. 1, Reports of John M. Richardson, 1 September 1848; 14 April 1848; Report of Rev. J. Schoenmakers, August 1848 [Serial 537].

U.S. Congress, 33rd Congress, 1st Session, House Document no. 1, Report of Andrew J. Dorn, 3 September 1853; Report of J. Schoenmakers, 1 September 1853 [Serial 710].

U.S. Congress, 33rd Congress, 2d Session, House Document no. 1, Report of Andrew J. Dorn, 31 August 1854; Report of Rev. J. Schoenmakers, 1 September 1854 [Serial 746].

U.S. Congress, 37th Congress, 2d Session, Senate Document no. 1, Report of W.G. Coffin, 2 October 1861; Report of P.P. Elder, 30 September 1861; Report of Rev. Paul M. Ponziglione, 2 September 1861.

U.S. Congress, 38th Congress, 2d Session, House Document no. 1, Report of W.G. Coffin, 24 September 1864; Report of P.P. Elder, 15 September 1864; Report of Rev. John Schoenmakers, 1 September 1864 [Serial 1220].

U.S. Congress, 40th Congress, 2d Session, House Document no. 103, Estimate of Appropriations to Defray Expenses of Osage Delegation to Washington, 16 January 1868 [Serial 1337].

U.S. Congress, 40th Congress, 3d Session, House Miscellaneous Document no. 49, Protest against Ratification of Sturgis [Drum Creek] Treaty, 15 February 1869 [Serial 1385].

U.S. Congress, Senate Committee on Interior and Insular Affairs, Subcommittee on Indian Affairs, Osage Nation of Indians Judgement Funds, Hearing, Ninety-Second Congress, Second Session, on S1456 and S3234, March 28, 1972, Government Printing Office: Washington, D.C., 1972. 3, 174.

Voget, Fred W., Osage Indians: Osage Research Project, Vol. 1 (American Indian Ethnohistory Ser.: Plains Indians), Garland Publishing, Inc.: New York.

White Horse Eagle, We Indians, New York, 1931. 255 pp.

Whitehouse, Joseph, "The Journal of Private Joseph Whitehouse, a Soldier with Lewis and Clark," ed. by Paul Russell Cutright, Missouri Historical Society, Bulletin, 28 (1971-1972): 143-161.

Williams, Alfred M., "The Giants of the Plain," Lippincott's Magazine of Popular Literature and Science, 32 (1883):362-371.

Woodstock Letters, The, 64 vols., Woodstock, Md., 1872-1935.

END NOTES

[1] Montagu, M.F. Ashley, "An Indian Tradition Relating to the Mastodon," American Anthropologist, New Series, v. 46, no. 4, 1944:568-571.

[2] La Flesche, Francis, "The Osage Tribe: Rite of the Chiefs; Sayings of the Ancient Men," Smithsonian, Bureau of Ethnology, 36th Annual Report, 1914-1915, Government Printing Office: Washington, 1921.

[3] Parkman, Francis, The Old Regime in Canada, Frontenac Edition, Little, Brown, and Company: Boston, 1899. (See pp. 11-27, Marriage and Population.)

[4] McGee, W.J., "The Siouan Indians: A Preliminary Sketch," Smithsonian, Bureau of Ethnology, 15th Annual Report, 1893-1894, Government Printing Office: Washington, 1897. (See pp. 187-189.)

C (cont.)

P (cont.)

Q

R

      (end of R)

S

T

www.ingramcontent.com/pod-product-compliance
Lightning Source LLC
Chambersburg PA
CBHW070422270326
41926CB00014B/2892